BY WANDA COLEMAN

Mad Dog Black Lady (1979)
Imagoes (1983)
Heavy Daughter Blues: Poems & Stories 1968–1986 (1987)
A War of Eyes and Other Stories (1988)
The Dicksboro Hotel (1989)
African Sleeping Sickness: Stories & Poems (1990)
Hand Dance (1993)
American Sonnets (1994)
Native in a Strange Land: Trials & Tremors (1996)
Bathwater Wine (1998)
Mambo Hips & Make Believe: A Novel (1999)
Love-ins with Nietzsche: A Memoir (2000)
Mercurochrome: New Poems (2001)

MER
CU
RO
CHR

WANDA COLEMAN

MERCUROCHROME

NEW POEMS

BLACK SPARROW PRESS • SANTA ROSA • 2001

ACKNOWLEDGMENTS

Several of these poems are continuations of numbered series, most of which appear in the author's previous collections. The author claims poetic license in her imitations and transliterations of poems from *The Contemporary American Poets: American Poetry since 1940,* edited by Mark Strand; and *Poems of Humor & Protest,* by Kenneth Patchen; with appreciation and gratitude to all others. Grateful acknowledgment is made to the editors of the following: *Another Chicago Magazine, Bomb, Bombay Gin, Dominion Review, The Drumming: Black Love & Erotic Poetry, Long Shot, Milk, The Outlaw Bible of American Poetry, Oxygen, Paterson Literary Review, Poetry International, Powerlines: A Decade of Poetry from Chicago's Guild Complex, Rattle, River City, River Styx, Solo, 306°: A Revolution of Black Poets, wake up heavy, The Washington Review, The World 56/77* (St. Mark's Poetry Project), and *X-Ray.*

Second Printing
Black Sparrow Press books are printed on acid-free paper.

LIBRARY OF CONGRESS CATALOGING-IN-PUBLICATION DATA

Coleman, Wanda.
   Mercurochrome : new poems / Wanda Coleman.
      p.   cm.
   ISBN 1-57423-153-7 (paperback)
   ISBN 1-57423-154-5 (cloth trade)
   ISBN 1-57423-155-3 (signed cloth)7
      I. Title.

   PS3553.O47447M4   2001
   811'.54—dc21   2001025242

In memory of Alan Rosen & Anthony Jerome Coleman

TABLE OF CONTENTS

MERCUROCHROME

New Poems

under your belly
there's gnawing in the bones
subterranean & abysmal
the bite that's more the unscratchable itch/coldfire
now he penetrates me against the landscape
of my own blood and demands escape from
the rotting tongue in which he's caged

this is the form i wear

out of my pernicious reason
and my slam-driven mind
comes the clay i shape into pleasures
for your knowing
the angles of his body
cut at my grasp-starved hands
his bone hard as young granite at my softness
the authority of his beauty demanding
the familiarity of my flesh

thus you hold me
frozen in your doubtful vision
in your study of my brownness. believe
my curious fingers. trust my
daring fingers
as they probe your opened wound
to find a roundness

I

CANNED FURY

nothing comes to mind. i am dispersed
on a page of ugly newsprint
the faraway noise of a child's cry
in the eleventh hour. i wait. it seems it

will take another five hundred years
this side of Eden
for shapelessness/to take form
and fashion. i wait. and the darkness stains

my eyes as i read
the fine print and footnotes. where
is my history/the full blood
minus bromides and falsities? who has

stamped happy faces
over my sorrow and broken erratic prose?

memory divides me against myself

without resolution. injunctions
from the court of public opinion
deny me access to the light.

my mother is plaintiff, her insurmountable rage
imprisons my heart

guilty. yes. i am as guilty as ever

never having quite awakened from sleep
indulging the molestations of The Sandman
encouraging a perverse and deepening
state of rimming. and having the nerve to
walk and talk/somnambulate in my discourse

what details shall be revealed when
the jailer sounds time to rise and shine?

imagination fails. all i see can be fondled
or broken. the ridiculous mattress with
its flesh-seeking springs, the thin itchy woolen
blanket thrown to the concrete. the steel
metal that tosses back my petulance

this stupid colorless uniform
is cut to fit a woman with no ass

there are no clocks here. the notion of time's
irrelevance is reinforced. spend your life
for little-to-no compensation. (yes. guilty
of nonconformity and the wickedness of high thought.)

settle into those mighty hips
like a tablespoon into semisweet chocolate dessert

i am an outlaw, they assert.
there's a ten-digit number stamped on my frontal lobe

i close my eyes to hear

joy. the terrible music of leaden wings
i am a child and tremble as i climb the ether

on my last day of heaven, i abandoned her womb
to claim my glory in her blood

there is no one here but me. from behind this glass
i see the guard's station. prisoners are watched
on TV monitors, a camera in each cell. if i move,
i see the wisp of my movement on the monitor.

i am here through no fault of my own as a result
of doing more for others than for myself. all the guards
are men. they can watch me undress and make my toilet.
they can watch me caress myself in my nightmares.

there is a pay phone in the prisoners' rec room
that does not take coins. communication is futile at worst,
faulty at best. i have learned that i am friendless.
no one has sympathy for me. i have learned
that misplaced trust can dismantle a life

as a result of this punishment, i have learned
it pays to be more selfish with desire.

memory divides me against the light

the body with tracks. the body on track. body tracks

i am blackness waking
my mother's face on my father's gift
i am the utter meaning
immeasurable, sensual and stark
i am the jetflow of subterranean events
my father's gentleness on my mother's savagery
i am blackness. the awakening

II

Twentieth Century Nod-Out

leads me through one overtaxed
little citytown
after gas stop after vista view,
eludes the gridlocked main highway,
avoids the rain-and-moon patrols and fiery
extinction on that hairpin curve
of credit and industry. i'm on the looksee
for that mean motor scooter,
one payment outracing the other
as i nightdrag cloud-lined bluffs toward
the destination i'm building on installments,
fingers crossed as i drive, double-malted in one hand,
French fries tucked against the armrest,
cheeseburger leaving grease stains
on the dashboard of my vision

back and forth the fire-haired cat/a trail
paw prints mark hood & trunk—a fever spikes at 106°
summons. the sentinels go

languid shudders come with evening's ruin
invisible planets offer themselves as red-orange stars
appear and circle the iris
as clouds invade the room
he lies in a brass bed
his Christmas robe unworn
the M&Ms unsealed. strains of Vivaldi
lilt on the compact disc player
guitar favorites on the sheet-music stand
lamps lit, TV screen dark. the male nurse aspirates
his dry gold mouth, his listless bloodless tongue

sentinels on guard in shock those hapless sentinels

it's sunset, my boys. guard the wind
be shocked at the rain. hate the ants

HOLLYWOOD THEOLOGY (2)

in this Gomorrah of Gomorrahs

one is forced to live up to whatever one eats

jacked up on zeal,
limited visionaries with partial
solutions abound, and all the winners are
stunned that defeat can shine so brightly

where sun-baked sallow-skinned madonnas
ride dashboards and blue chip stamps promise
middle class nirvana
where the wise speak in monotones

the media has been infiltrated by
midnight movers, those bone-packing
desperadoes of The New Disorder

and all the intellectuals are walking
around with Boy Scout knives
buried in their brains

while over three hundred corpses a year
are found quietly rotting in Griffith Park

(our cops can beat up your cops)

where frequent violations
of the outlawed ritual of public toking
indicate lack of fiber during
a past incarnation of the bowel

lost between the book the game & the crack
mailfolk and census statisticians

keep finding themselves victims to
pit bulls & wrong-way drivers

revamped religions thrive on confused
believers in prefabricated love,
and a sense of purpose is this week's disease
symptomatic of dislocation trauma

    (sins borrowed for entertainment ugliness
    made holy & useful, devoid of
    forgiveness. you. fathamutha)

these streets are filled with insomniacs
and the detritus of defrocked breeders
excuse & endurance mingle as meek jesuses
practice obscene finger worship

rebirth here is all sequins, nail enamel & smoke

lilacs you picked
passing thru
a pepper tree among the rocks,
Chinese lantern in the yard. diplomacy in
dream corridors/a meeting

leading to your door

close scrutiny come to pass,
notion gone awry
two thieves
a parting comment, truth
inquire yet desire
tellingly

past the flats

wanderer, a faraway market
writings on a tree trunk
in a village one night

wake me not

a rustic scene, away from winter's chill
a quiet window. yearn
the late night wind, a python's coil
as you danced a sharing

a red man by the lake
a scorching black crucible
blood on fire
the uncommon flight

mainstream statistics are correct. i know
their tallies in my browner flesh
there's no future but an echo within an echo
and as i lay me down to pray (perhaps some
minor fire for this dragon left to spray?),
some other dog has snatched my glory's day.

and what is left is willful wreck that sinks
and stinks beneath its sumptuous lusty weight/
that's ripe for salvage or sewage in current's
undertow. oh there but for the grace smile i. how
sweet the lilacs but i only smell the lie.

spare moi
the naughty finger shaking shame my way
until you've slumbered my skin you've
nothing worth your vicious effort's say
i think it true to observe, well damn! the sun is hot!
and blow one's nose when fever's caught
	and running snot

so leave me with my arrows and my slings
that i may go about the work of zinging things

the thief has made me a gift of his night's booty

somewhere, a daughter discovers her mother's coral
brooch missing. somewhere, a man recoils at the absence
of his gambling stash. somewhere, a miser riles
over a vanished ransom in newly minted silver

all this to buy a hotbed of memories
to feed the children fresh-killed lies
to open all the locks on love

forever is a moment we hold in our stomachs

as he brushes the smudge of his kiss
across my lips, i smell the cologne of his fear
a robust and smoky aroma mingled
with the woody musk of courtrooms and the stench of
pain-paved alleyways

i take these things and promise to stay mum

there's anxious talk of dreadful blaze
of fortitude that brings not one whit
    of satisfaction
the revenues of bawlings
    death by exaggeration

fairgender demands surrender
in the tenderness of attire
    softness bends the metal
and fiendish roots flee the sun
    and everything that seems
natural, leaves savage splendor's
    mark on tender flanks

a brute's paw
to be worn as reminder
when bending to pluck a rose
the rose must look behind her

my days lengthen with sullen sorrow
when time bids me grief's banishment
our excessive cushes & congress
    (the lizard's wife)
and in my end the giant lappings
heaven's lust visits this—my dusky realm
and dives for pink-and-glowing pearl
where rich in the fortune of
his brazen wand/his glory's way
makes mine beauty's shriek
to do his good his beast imbogged
    at axis. first husht
in pleasure's immediacy he trumpets
    dark as knowledge,
    hard as forever, the
treasure of his thrust denying measure

it's a verb drives verb world

where she huddles in his exhaust, tiny & deformed
governed by a flow of wonts

everything that runs on adjectives is stalled

street crimes abound—the bump & run of fast gab
trunk thefts gagas drive-bys gagas snipings

    warning!
don't lower your windows for well-dressed talk
don't stop in a residential zone to still sudden
    stutters
develop a protective code of tongue when
one's vocabulary is arrested for DUI
act as if being possessed by adverbs is an everyday
    affair. don't
complain that the noun is too tight. keep
the eyes dotted. don't volunteer a syllable.

as for homonym invasions & trope jackings
avoid being a victim, remember: blowouts may
cause permanent syntax damage. stay in the right lanes
should a quick exegesis be mandatory

(pronounce it aloud, once, for yourself. put
a breath at the end of each sentence, thus
sustaining the wordsmith who may wag & wax
anew. speak in even tones, in a language so poor
it wouldn't pay to steal a phonon)

    this

a survivor's whine to sweet soft grammars
coupled with rhetorical purrs—held
neological hostage to used word dealers

chance driving on the rim of meaning. it's cheaper
to replace than a presumed sanity

full speed. blues ahead

an infant's cry broken by a hiss

wheals rising on skin at the apparition of a thought

the hanged man the inverted moon the devil's tower
(all in one draw)

the hasty sweepings of a broom echoing against cement
just before sunrise

muffled snores escaping down pillows
at the mahogany head of a bed emptied of dreamers

whispers of
coffee stains on white sheet rock walls

blood wells clotting in a petulance

the remnants of a free-wheeling expanding
democracy are revealed in the high polished
wooden beamed ceiling, and only the vague spooks of a
crowded downtown thoroughfare. it's all squirreled
down by the miserly greed of a cheapskate generation

plastic, Formica & Styrofoam
quick mean political fixes & a pill for grandness

listen. there's the sure brace of a woman's
high-heeled step, nearly a march, hips swinging,
the confident swish of a skirt,
on her way to round up late-night arrivals by train

above, there's the gravel & grate of wind through
age-worn pipes. the shallow whistle of air
through conditioning ducts

i sit in the tan leather-upholstered high-backed
chairs made for monarchs and for children who
get a thrill when
their feet can't touch ground

there are a handful of students, weary commuters,
but mainly impatient drivers eager to get on
with pedestrian routines.
to close it down for the night

behind me sit two wood-colored men who smell
of backrooms & bourbon
in slag-colored duds and workshoes. they mark
time, suppress their nicotine fits
"smoke these days and they'll put yo' ass in jail"

laugh-broken, they assess the "stupid young muthafuckas,"
with a "they must be out of their mixed-up
don't know what to do minds."

that could be said of the city officials
who have allowed this magnificence to decay
(as better the best go fallow & fail than
to let us have it or any true say in it)
and uh-huh at the irony. me and brutha men whose
tone i echo would not have been welcomed on
these premises in that heyday one mean lifetime ago

the sweet Eisenhower simmer was toughest
harsh blurrings/a vicious & unforgiving nature
descending on the city in a rain of heat
roasting resolve alive

(be out of Heaven by sundown, niggah)

i remember the childhood allure of chiffon
flowing from broad bronze shoulders
pastel pill-box hats with peek-a-boo veils
perched on crowns slick-pressed to Sunday,
Sugar Ray by night—Tootsweet by day

summer came draped in Hawaiian cotton print
muumuus & Italian-heeled slip-ons
rattling pukka shell bracelets, lobes armed
with sterling silver hoops

hey fandango

a curious shaking under the palms
fine frames hugged in Playtex & leopard skin

gaunt-eyed men with big brown bones
biting the lips off unlit stogies
in brown suits behind the wheels of tore-down
coupes whistling the promise off billboards
as they swooped star-lined boulevards

i recall all of that smothered in
an untested belief in all things possible
as hard as fresh as raspberry ripple

i knew a soft boy once

he lived across our street. in time,
i did not like him because he was soft
in all the wrong places.
he was blacker than me, like Dutch chocolate
but didn't seem to know the hurtful names
people called me. if i complained,
"sticks & stones" he'd say.
"but," i argued, "words have as much power to kill
and maim as stone."
"shades of gray," he'd grin as i laid pain out
in black and white.
"each to his..." he'd yawn when i described
a world of abuse. i wanted empathy & tea leaves,
answers & directions toward a healing path.
he rolled his eyes and waxed, "the grapes of..."

i wanted to incite in him fire and indignation,
the desire to protect
but he just looked at me, clucked his tongue
and scratched his neck

we call him Olmec, my round-headed little
boy with wise wonderful old countenance
a Buddha-head, dark yellow cut with
a dash of red—profiling like a half besotted
sun against the full. his Negroid nose
is my nose. but that startled abused child
who fathered him, looks slyly back at me from
time-to-time. we ride together, side by side
and i occasionally ask him what he remembers
of his early days. like that morning the
locked car door flew open, on the way to school,
and he flew out, and i suffered
the fragmented horror of having crushed him
under the Buick's right gangster white
sidewall steel-belted radial. he recalls that
uncanny instant, he says, and more....
we muse softly together under the music he loves
as he takes me by the ears and guides me back
through a tangle he could not know, when
i still secretly *believed*, and was happy, and
then the rock guitar angel unexpectedly
strums and whines steel blues about us, snapping
me back into our present and i startle my
darling with the oblation of his conception

the doctors found a strangeness in my children
and called in the specialist from Sweden, who looked
them over and declared, "Ahhh. Please, note this odd
webbing of the hands and feet. Ahhh. These spots of skin
discoloration. Ahhh. This unusual elongation of the
extremities. Ahhh. Such curvature of the spinal column!
Run chromosomal analyses and heat topographies! Brain
            scans,
quickly! X-ray their backs! Biopsy their hearts!"

when the results of the tests were made available,
he studied them.
i awaited his report with dread. at last,
we spoke and he gave me the results of his examination.

"These are not children," he asserted. "These are elephants.
Soon they will grow enormous tusks of ivory and will
            develop
trunks where they now have noses. The earth will tremble
when they walk. This is a serious matter. In a short time,
they will become far too dangerous for mundane
            containment,
demanding a significant amount of nourishment and
            attention."

"And then," he whispered "there exists
the very serious potential of stampede."

1

i was not born. i was invented

stark & raving
relying heavily upon my cultural heritage
of poverty & bad grammar

my stumblings across the human landscape

(i didn't start out
              to be an ink spot)

all my loves massacred (mother, 'no hawk's blood was e'er
so red') in an unseemly rush to dignity

my identity as a speaker of dreams
& ceremonies in dark cold thoughts

words like wild ponies freed to roam southwestern plains

sympathy reserved for the prophets, profligates
and pollyannas touting false positives

while my cruel & perverse sense of justice
incites riots of exoticism—broken minds, shattered fictions

living in a white sensibility
(there are no dirty sentences here)

blues (my deep sense of inexorable limitations)
expressed in my will to conquer
this nationally sanctioned villainy
spirited to the weary-witty last

i too have cried i am, but have gathered nothing
but a strange unforgiving silence

2

of an unfortunately undereducated caste
self-cultivated and self-promoted
too thick to surrender (bullhearted)
this lightness and basin spell the tomb.
what am i to say when my temple is desecrated
and the shitter goes unclean and unpunished?
i am cut off from friends & fans, locked
in the ghetto of my extra-societal failures
ill-supported in my apostolic depression
unpatronized & unpampered, rags-to-rags
an unconventional American (skkkugly)
sardonic & powerless in my empty purse
eyes ogleless, flesh violating the limits of nylon.
nothing here but the rubble of high hopes
the dust of collapse choking off breath.
i am slipping from my own grasp
there rises a soul-sickening despair
and i pray that i will not survive the fall

3

imprisoned in the sugar bowl

ant. i couldn't keep the job i thought i wanted. ant.
what does an angelic shade like me do in Hades?
(i felt moved by my own sense of life. was that
irrational?)

antantant. true ant

trapped in an adolescent fantasyland where
garbage is plentiful as evidence of gluttony yet legions starve

(it took godzillion years for that pissant to notice me
sitting on his face. and now
all he can do is express the silly regret that he
didn't bother to notice me before my cherry was popped)

in this strange revolt where i loot sentences
for sustenance

ant. and more ant

"we cannot escape our organs no matter how hard we try,"
    said The Gypsy

mediocrity & cowardice of barbaric proportions
occlude the consciousness of my generation. ant

beware any tendency to substitute kneejerk approval
for a profound if exothermic understanding

red ant

unfulfilled. wasted. sweet as raw sugar. untasted

wham. blue ant

i do not visit my father's grave often enough
so he visits me

i hear his voice of which there is no recording

his last day his last breath has not been forgotten
i reassure him

i stare at the picture of him in my mind
i talk to him. he tells me everything will be another
thing. he's freshly showered, his hair is greased back with
Murray's pomade,
he's wearing his favorite pinstripe suit
a crisply starched white shirt, black silk tie &
hanky to match,
black silk socks and black patent leather shoes

he knows half my heart is lying when i say i'm proud
to have inherited his hair

i apologize for not being able to make that last reunion
the one in Arkansas

he is saddened that i am so unhappy
he regrets that i have so many troubles but
has confidence that i will handle them

he knows it didn't bother me that he wasn't always
faithful. he knows i understand men—now

but on the other hand, he knows
we are still staring anxiously from phone to door
waiting half the night for him to come home

dinner is spoiled

he accepts my forgiveness for all the spankings
except one.
he knows i've also inherited his stubborn nature
and his weakness for warmth

he has forgiven my prank of putting salt in the sugar bowl

dear Georgiana,

  there are few secrets left to keep
  they leave me like shedding skin
  after one of my horrible weeping rashes
  for which there was no cure, only
  the long soaks and the damp towels and
  the averted eyes of thwarted care. there
  was no fearless child to play with so
  i'd stew in my agony in front of the
  TV console, home sick from school,
  not seeing the screen but staring
  beyond it to some future moonrise
  transported into space by stubborn will
      to
  a blister-free happiness manned by
  a valiant conk-haired dreamdaddy
      to
  that utopia/that white-on-white paradise
  where the enamel glistens and i'm push-button
  perfect, all aglimmer and blank-eyed
  in my padded bra & spotless pink apron
  all canary yellow latex-rubber manbait

  sister

  is there too much time between us?

her profile & three-quarters of an eye
peer off-canvas
perfect lime calabash slices of sorrow hang
at one geometrically suspect see-thru breast
with mauve-toned nipple
right beneath the strangled cucumbers that shape
a hand, fanning full flag, there's a slight
but irrepressible squiggle
like a blade broken off on a rib
or half mustache lost mid-tickle

she is here. can she come in?

dear Georgiana,

i'm sorry i haven't written till now
but i'm terribly embroiled
and i'm having these headaches caused by grinding
my teeth in my sleep. plus all the bullsquat
as usual. i want so much to be involved
in worthy causes, but i can barely manage to
keep the hand to the mouth.
i hate disappointing friends & potential
friends. i haven't had a party in years. i owe
scads of people invitations and am unable
to return them. it's very hard
to put one thought in front of the other.
i had to force myself to work tonight. a hissy fit
overcame me. i toughed through it. i'm here
by myself. i hated to pick up the phone.
who would i call? who wants to hear it? who
has the time? who isn't burnt out?
so i worked worked worked till the furious
tears dried up. i kept remembering
that scene in *A Streetcar Named Desire*—you
know the one?—where Blanche DuBois
is about to be taken away and
flutters against the dinginess of that dirty
window like a moth trapped in a mad gleam.
that scene plays over and over
in what's left of my mind.
o sis, i work and i work and take
aspirin for the headache and drink coffee to
fight off drowsiness and take a bite of
something sweet for the sugar rush.
i still believe in myself. and i want to do

my best to honor those, like yourself,
who no longer have the privilege of work

yes. it is getting late. i'll close. i hope you
don't resent my sharing this sort
of stuff with you. but
you know how it is with Mother....

dear people

this is a fabulous human interest
    story
about a northern California town's
efforts to survive when threatened
by post earthquake development proposals
from county, state & federal bureaucrats
    which chronicles
the town's unsuccessful fight against
    corrupt
officials whose financial schemes
irreparably alter their idyllic
    boheme life style

important issues are raised as
    a let-well-enough-
alone policy toward marijuana cultivation
    becomes no-smoke
and the rich economic subculture
is threatened. a free health clinic
where acupuncture, holistic medicine
and abortions are provided to low
income residents is bombed, killing
two of the town's top cancer researchers
and a volunteer cosmetic surgeon, whose
widow is also the town's mayor

griefstricken, she resigns from office
    and a wealthy
conservative realtor with Mafia ties
is elected in close (fixed) race with
the mayor's twenty-eight-year-old son, a poet

and journalist known for his hot
investigative pieces on contemporary
sociopolitical issues. it is our
        belief
that

we were never caught

we partied the southwest, smoked it from L.A. to El Dorado
worked odd jobs between delusions of escape
drunk on the admonitions of parents, parsons & professors
driving faster than the road or law allowed
our high-pitched laughter was young, heartless &
            disrespected
authority. we could be heard for miles in the night

across the Grand Canyon of new manhood,
womanhood discovered
like the first sighting of Mount Wilson

we rebelled against the southwestern wind

we got so naturally ripped, we sprouted wings,
crashed parties on the moon, and howled at the earth

we lived off love. it was all we had to eat

when you split you took all the wisdom
and left me the worry

befuzzment
those assassins' bullets tore through our skulls
splattered the brains of our courageous fortune
all over the TVland tuck & roll
sent all-American youths into decades of
post-traumatic stress syndrome
the sun of our future forever eclipsed
betrayal was rampant as
disillusionment denial denigration
    set in
tora tora tora was declared against
the naive the sincere & the mental/a silent
napalming stateside as the cities
became demilitarized zones

(you will get your effing freedom niggahs
wiggahs and what-have-yous left of center
    but
it will be nulled & ungroovy
as failure & reversals become a way
of suspended animation—life
at its least if not fullest denied in an
avalanche of drugs disease & moral downsizing

you will either surrender, conform
or suck God)

june   the starlings have eaten the cat

june   rereading *Trilce*

june   psychic snow fell last night,
an outside transmission. an old
passion was cloaked in a new
philosophy

june   agate eyes were found under the pillow.
slow to warm

june   the exhausted controversy refuses resolution

june   when i went to rake up the disgusting
fur ball, i found a dead baby possum

june   my eyes hurt

june   the interloper is leaving shit
all over my life

june   spent the evening talking to the walls.
nobody showed, not even my guest list.

june   watched *Gilda* one hundred and sixty-five times

june   they say i should forgive America, but
they're the ones hiding behind
bulletproof glass

june   the squirrels have eaten the plumber

she keeps her napkins in the veggie bin, her
panty hose in the deep freeze

a gaggle of geese gathers under the wool
of an apolitical matronage against
the pastoral green of a muzzled intelligence

media panjandrums wigglin' apander

originality taxes memory
and, like everything experienced, religion
is material

perpetuation of a plaguing purposelessness
the logic of kissing: solve equate transmit

(the anthology niggers are galumphing for
       greatness
upping no divvy to contributors as they
piggyback their ways to tenured glory)

beware. in your coming of age you may
discover you are the damned & dreaded darkling

when you lock it in, tear off the knob

nothing in this meat grinder, Lovey
but sheep and Judas goats

dear Greenie,

there are those who have no passion but who
are sensitive enough to sense the void within
and therefore must imagine passion. i often find
that among that kind, there are those who
detest the truly passionate out of an envious rage

that has always faced us passionate ones. ever will

a man who is jailed for his passion gone awry
arouses in his kindred a simple but deep
compassion. for we, too, reside in our own inward
jails built of the conflicts passion inspires

we clang at our bars in silence, out of public view

like Paul said, you can't judge the depth
of a man's passion by looking into his eyes. it comes
on the aura of the skin, resides on the throne
of presence, crackles on his breath
as with a woman as in a woman's heart-eye

likewise is the display in a spectrum of tones
and not merely the cliche of purple

(sort of gives new context to one-eyed purple
people-eaters, doesn't it?)

it has always struck me funny,
that often the least passionate people are poets,
contrary to myth. perhaps it's a case
of the poet giving all there is of passion

to the verse leaving those who hunger
outside it sucking up air

i've certainly been a witness to
the kind of passionless entity who must create
chaos out of calm
and thence extract the passion
from the moment with the forceps
of their ravenous intellect—prodding, pulling
and causing everything delicate to bleed

giving no consequence to damage. because now
they have the passion from which to shape the poem

i'm sure you're familiar with that kind of psyche

so in your retreat, consider—those drawn to
Just Plain God-awful Poetry are not only drawn to it
out of ignorance, but to the pools of unskillfully
spilled passion they find brimming in the tongue

they are distance-sick, made ill by the world
in which violent passions are subsumed/made perverse/
outlawed. they are made ill by the word turned in on itself
as constraint against release/dangerous abandon

i am always struck by the "safe" poetry
the most bloodless, banal crap i've ever had
the misfortune to read assembled out of the
need for foundation money, the fear of risk,
the need to be free of dolor, to create,
these pathetic versifiers have drained all
passion from their words—the lustful
or the didactic—lest they be rejected. or
in peripheral ways, oblique and skewed.
one is forced to plow through reams

of coming-of-age musings and death-dying
musings and musings mundane and stale.
reams and reams of the cutesy-wootsy
the wootsy-pootsy and the gamesteristic

so that by the end of the process one is dying
to pick up a page of Jeffers, Kaufman or Poe

Keats for Kkkkristsakes

go to a movie—anything to get
neck-deep in some goodlikkity trash
because that's where the passion
is dicking around fresh and alive and
delivered on a paper plate seeping grease
yet honest in its salty pleasure

hot baloney and American cheese

that's why i find it so difficult to critique
poetry. i realize that passion seeks its own heat
so to speak. and that the bardic bad serves in its way
as well as the good. E. B. Browning or Edna St. V

then, Greenie,

there are those like me besotted with passion
when touched lightly passion oozes
to the skin's surface and runs earthward
passion leaks from ears eyes mouth gummy with passion
crusting at the lips clothes passion-stained and
unwashable passion in every step and gesture *pashzuhn*
overcome and overwhelmed and sickened by and
with it. passion. and desperate for the soul-letting

given no consequence

say. look. i know you
don't do this sort of thing
but. say. Laura Nyro wants to see you
she's gonna be in town. you know. touring
for her newest release.
she's feelin' kinda sick
but she's in good form. a little heavy. now.
but, you know how it is

mama. i'm on a cane myself.
the lights are dim at McCabe's for folk & blues
guitar-covered walls & the ghost of Fay Wray

we enjoy, sometimes sing along
to show-flavored rag-tinged tunes (Laura as
spirit artist in this shooksorry world.) it's solid,
her best/an offering as she takes us down
that Stoney End

afterwards,
we go upstairs for props & Chinese

we say grace. i cop, say i'm a fan
she praises me for the poem
i thank her for the song

it's her last tour, her last visit to Los Angeles
we touch, hug and nod

soon the light will darken over Danbury

mama cradle her again

friends as the smoke ash drops
till all the clocks in heaven stop
giggles and an accounting of tragedies
no shortage of stories to exchange
youth is out of range and we are free-dangling
women in a realm fixed on adolescence
our potential & talent squandered by the stupidity
    of certain men
who couldn't see beyond what tits & ass we had
and now, we disappear right before their eyes
erased as if our days had never been
she is fat and i am thin
friends as the smoke ash drops
and all the clocks in heaven stop
wonder at the miracles that we still breathe
no shortage of miseries to exchange
glory is out of range and we are free-dangling
women in a nation fixed on silliness
our ability & beauty ignored by the stupid
who can't see beyond what fills our purse
and now, we go poof! right before their eyes
because our days have never been
i am fat and she is thin
friends as the smoke ash drops
and all the clocks in heaven stop

THE LADY IN THE RED VEILED HAT

—for Laurel Ann Bogen

yes. it's insanity
writing poetry in Los Angeles

but something significant has happened here

ask the voluptuous lady in the red veiled hat
she'll tell you. follow her. late one evening, along
avenues and boulevards as she cruises
for the indefinable/as she prowls dingy digs and viperous
venues seeking that elusive moment when the words
ignite the heart. ask the voluptuous lady
in red, smile cloaked in diaphanous fire. she'll tell
you about the petty jealousies, the infighting,
the backbiting, the scuffles at the mike. ask that
lusty lady in the red hat with orbs like sirens.
she'll tell you about the loneliness,
the neglect, the disappointments, the lies
ask her. ask her if you dare!

o lady in the red hat. your sable hair. your pale flesh
your lips painted into a wound

when they ask you
about the razor blades you swallowed
tell them they were less dangerous than the abuse
dealt by low-down lovers afraid of creative allure
when they ask you
about pills and stomach pumps
tell them there's no cure for the metaphors and
similes coursing thru your blood

when they ask you
about the scars crossing your wrists
describe your wicked escapes thru shattered eyes
when they ask you
about the night, tell them
it has joined you

dream-stung lady in the red veiled hat
you've kept your secrets far too long. o lady
in the red veiled hat, we need your selfish beauty
we need your vision, your voice. we need your words

those pulsating dramas that catch the breath
that throb in the groins of the jaded

snapping

a warped sense of communication
impairs the business of conventional narrative

like feeling robbed, the rules of orgasm no mystery

given a voice, one must struggle with one's own
social type-casting on the edge of ambiguity

it's exclusively inconclusive

(language cannot contain this magnitude of afro-agony.
righteous rage is difficult to keep jacketed)

snapping. not a march (on Washington or anywhere else),
but a death ballet

i am compelled to protest
the demise of the deliciously clandestine.
the new underground is sterile,
devoid of dangerous rhythms, and strewn
with the grotesque bones of riotous fists

downed birds. thru the art
                thru the art

(looks as desolate as a chassis graveyard)

repeated midnight embraces. yet i've slipped
out of the framework of love
lost confidence. all these years wasted.
no lucrative controversy on the literary horizon

(the centaur bends over me, towers. release
in the blade of his tongue)
issuing from the culture

one bullet and a nation bleeds for decades
speaking of dragging out a bad ending

what neither illuminates nor exemplifies/corrodes
grappling with onset of antipoetics
badly mangled intent and didactic syntax

alas. i may never find the proper adverb

snapping

hiding the face after it makes
front page news

straightening out a bent disposition

killer shadows armed with nasty gats
chasing down a rat on the eve of righteousness

wise & ultimate peace

squeezing the three-hundred pound lady
into the size ten life

rising out of the dungheap unstained

he looks the part. trying
to make him play it

finding a cure for October

dear Georgiana,

    trying to do something to shake off this
        post holiday boohoohoo.
as you know, i've been poking at baby sis again.
        she looks like
strawberry shortcake, but watch the hardtack
        underneath. it'll
crack your teeth. it would be victory over
        raging hearts
should we manage to become friends. but that's
        going to take more
vital stuff than i have to bleed. put that on hold.

    besieged and collapsing under the weight
        of my gift. love
as i live it seems more like Mercurochrome
        than anything else
i can conjure up. it looks so pretty and red,
        and smells of a balmy
coolness when you uncap the little applicator.
        but swab it on an
open sore and you nearly die under the stabbing
        burn. recovery
leaves a vague tenderness and an India ink-red
        splotch that'll
vanish between one scrubbing or another

    Mama's favorite lipstick used to be a sultry
        red violet
that segued into the hue of sangria when
        applied to her
full rose-brown lips. i liked watching her

              slick moves as
she studied her face over the dressing
              table mirror, but
best was how she briskly slipped it
              from her purse
while sitting in the car, cupping her compact
              in one palm while
she uncapped the tube with a flick. One twist
              of the brass
canister's butt, and the stick rose for duty

the pangs-n-thangs of girlhood are foremost on my
              agenda of items suppressed.
they storm the Barrier Reef of my consciousness
              like shipwrecked
swabbies, drunk with trauma, washed inland to
              a grimmer death
against the shore where rent flesh, first red,
              turns salt white

someone drives. there are fingers pointing.
he sits beside me. we are cruising north Vermont for
an automatic teller machine
looking for the new branch of our ever-changing bank.
the driver pulls over and i hop out and accidently
wipe out my account, which only has two hundred smackers
left. i take the cash and slip it into my bag

he disappears, as does the driver

later, i am somewhere else. i park the Skylark in the shade,
forgetting to take my purse
when i return much later, the sky is overcast & windy
the windows on the Skylark are rolled down,
the interior covered in dried brown leaves.
beneath them, i find my black leather tote in the backseat
and reach for it, brush away the leaves, survey the deserted
                street.
relieved, i unzip my coin pouch and find
all the money inside untouched

in his handsomeness, he reaches through my slumber
and wakes me with a kiss sunnyside up

the finale starts when Blondie fires the cannon
and you tumble and stumble into an arena of tombs
at the end of your rogue's quest where
a life's fortune is interred in a nameless grave
(next to Arch Stanton). you run and you run!
an exquisite circular ballet of raw happy greed
(the kind i feel when i read the well-written)
as the bells & sopranos crescendo. then,
you spade the dust with a broken cross
to discover the bones of a scene-stealing
performance. it is the dance that you do
that i wait and watch for, my eyes
tasting the sweat on your brow, riding the
impish tilt of your bearded bravado.
it's a grand bang-bang spaghetti shoot-'em-up
and when the smokin' lead no longer flies
Angel Eyes (the bad) will be dead, Blondie
(the good?) will scam you with a ruse
a noose and his sharpshooter's aim. but
the last line rings and will always be yours
after you bump your head on a dreamlaced rock
        only to jump
to your boots and let go a swear that tells him
        he hit the bull's-eye.

some infidels never dry up. they remain moist
even on the fire

quote me. let me hang on your lips, ecstasy
        renewed. or like oil
glistening as if the painter had just stepped back
        into a better light
        a brush stroke away

no one (you must whisper) can take you from me
as i've taken you from other loves & lovers

my eyes so greedy
see myself in yours, radiant with sweat & seed

the air is laced with scratch fever & moolaflu
    abruptly it is late
and spores swim in on the trills of forgotten squeals
    the maiden has become the ma'am
trapped in the nightmares of the child abandoned for the job
    the monster has come, truer monster
    demise a privilege to date denied
as her lover grapples to hold her here, earthstitched

she rises, sunstruck
(can anyone so blacksouled survive this whiteness?)

multiple rebirth is
the option eschewed
for reconstruction,
becoming daring enough
desirable enough, cured
of confidential horror
or science faction

can one embellish or exaggerate the autoeroticism
of slit vision?

surreal violet enamels the fake sky
and down from it rains a marrow-cracking heat
    in the calamity
brains slam-dance on windshields as if during gridlock
ears blues-starved for melodic fingerings
(worst they could say about her after she's gone? nothing)

her lover hustles to hold her here
couplings perverse in their intensity & frequency
gluing her back together with his meat

a hateful hot spring night
the enormous spider climbs her eternal web
the white blossoms poison the night breeze
the tall horrors crowd my loneliness
the moon is black the sky is black
     black cat with yellow eyes
i am terrified of my shadow
he appears in the driveway. he slams the car door.
     his eyes
embittered by our nightmare, he stumbles
toward the steps. he enters this white house.
his rude silence stains the cheap sheetrock walls.
     nooselike, his tie hangs
from around his stiff collar. distractions spread
     like grease
off hot meat to the bottom of a pan. when will
the jealous world leave us alone?
when will the dream free us? when will the rain
     of debt cease?
i dab away salt with the edges of my apron.
i prepare a simple supper of fowl, peas and rice.
     thoughts of duns
bleed the sex from my groin. black cat
     with yellow eyes
my feet skip mindlessly about. they, too,
     are terrified

giving birth to soft white shoulders aching
bruise—a man who's bad news
a needle to tattoo poems/hearts
a collection of yellowing complaints tenuously
held on pages by the dry tape of her hunger
she wants to eat up the world
(it's difficult to digest, keeps threatening
to be vomited up, causes eyes to bulge,
convulses the thorax, invades the nose
endangers the living room rug)
letters praise/reject/play safe
mother-smiles, understanding is a salon
appointment away. she's birthed an artist
whose eyes dance between suicide and murder
scissors, snips of paper, reviews & articles
testify as red as blood or dried dark roses
she turns the page, finds herself glued there
curled up like a lock of hair
fetal and very readable under lamplight

winter my beloved

like our hair, our dreams are going gray
the stars are winking out
first a father, then a child, an uncle—and soon,
others, including a mother or two
who will be left to care or carry on?

a chill in the bowel

here we are divided from comfort by lies
and stubborn jealousies/the hateful manias
fed by ancient rivalries & misreadings
(who was most loved? who was punished or spanked
for every niggling mistake? who was deprived
of childhood? who most desperately seized the night?)

a dulling of the reflexes

there is no rescue. the larder
is full of moths. little white moths like
annoying flits of decay. there is no luck. chaos
steals our sleep, crisis robs us of time & cash

brittle nails & thoughts

hours crawl yet weeks fly
bones spit and curse bad steps
first slow then slower. light hurts.
strange noises confuse the ears. bruises
refuse to heal. the pose causes muscle strain

numbness & tingling

winter my beloved
nothing made of flesh is safe

they will arrive by helicopter before noon
the authorities will send them among us
they will storm our neighborhoods and cordon off
    connecting streets
they will come in camouflage helmets and suits
their tenderness protected by flakjackets
hands raised to halt the suspicious & the innocent

you'd better come unarmed. you'd better walk
with your hands
where they can see them

    no strong lingo allowed
    nothing outside their experience allowed
    no access without sanction

this age-old enemy is not playing games
the object of this action is to silence
displacement & relocation will take place later
executed by high-bottomed bureaucrats
after the superficial fires of controversy have died
and the media has resumed its indifference

this existence is voided
run if you must. but beware the circle

nirvana-found prematurely, Who Me swung from
a knotty participle this morning, book bolted
from the inside, context sealed tight. homicide
detected little other than cookie crumbs, a week-old
bag of cracklings and a moldy POV. grounds stuck at
the bottom of a red coffee mug, ink-stained sheets,
sweat-soaked bandana and spittle-damp doobies
also quickly proved nowhere clues. the nosey dame
one-wall-over swears-by-jequirity she heard an
argument and tusslings punctuated by blood-curdling
howls which aroused indifference since howls
from Who Me recurred with piercing frequency

true mystery?

suicide uptown catty-waggers dare
cry others crosstown 'twas murder-so-fair

every minor breeze seems to whisper Chinese

coroner's report reads demise by accidental
suspension from own plot device

gargantuan effort bags hurt-stained eyes,
heat-cracked teeth and back spasms at the overstress
    of a vowel. chaos
has settled in and made itself to home
a concerto of coughs & moans fortissimo—rood music
    for the cash bereft
as titans clash in the space of a Hollywood toilet,
whamming psyches into last week.

it's another day of dancing at the holocaust
the same ol' cold-blooded bloodlessness
enervating the unlucky the weak the poor—jes
another mundane bash to inspire upper-class yawns

the four horsemen have capped the fortune five-hundred
and the apocalypse is in the mail

and the crows go by...

my teacher revealed a pattern
a black shaft loomed up inside me and grew bigger
as night grew
yet i leave this earth a lowly eater
without having tasted good meat
in this neutered air where mad Nijinskys swoon
in ambidextrous ennui
better to have never been born than to die ignored

> mistress of slumber
> white sleep
> bloodfire (my breasts swollen and itchy
> with his suckings)

America, i broil in the racism which makes
me who i am—just another dead voice
without a booking agent

i have learned how women fall to bone
how true women suffer what false men celebrate

these ravings in my ear come off the yap
of a faithless friend

in this dark time brave tongues are mute
in this field of cinders i am the smoke
my genius turned ferocity

i fall down on my knees and beg

my son's terrible eyes
my son's terrible eyes and sad cold hands

whatever you were looking for is not here
nor was it—here—from the beginning
whatever you thought it was it is not
and no attempt was made to deceive you

there were no inner reaches for you to explore
except those you imagined and projected
given the limits of your life experiences
and the corset of your biases

your need is its own creator

whoever told you otherwise had plans of their own
and neglected to inform you that you were
being used. whoever told you otherwise
did you no favors and will not return yours
if asked

if you have wondered if there's a place
for you in all of this, wonder further if
there's a place for anyone who does not seize
& feed with a fierceness to rival death

think about generosity. then measure out what
yours has gotten you

when you bump your head on an unseen hardness
in the blindness, think about kindness
and all it has earned

it will find me unprepared
hair messed up
teeth unbrushed
one shoe on the wrong foot
in dirty underwear
papers scattered from hem to horizon

screaming obscenities as i
chase around some unfinished business
with an aerosol can of bugkill

no. i will never be ready to remember anything
but the afterimages of my children

maybe his power perhaps his husbandly arms
circling me, our coming sweetly one
the drops of his sweat to my cheek
how the air cools in our heat

otherwise

i'm done with reading. all thumb-worn books closed

there is nothing left for me in this macrocosm
it has ruined me with its greedy taking
a thankless adolescence stealing all
my treasures, violating my faith
embittering my thoughts, ridiculing my blackness

starting here. i turn around
and glimpse the abominations i've withstood
and the scars i will carry
until i'm a scab on Azrael's ass

i'm not ready now and will never be
for this moment this cathexis this

knocking within the skull

demise came undignified & unfashionably
as we went crashing, airborne through a hilly overgrowth
of water-drenched dichondra in a black-on-black sedan
a tangle of twisted mettle and shattered smiles

the sun was magenta, the sky was maroon
the stars spelled out my name

i was young & pregnant, again/overly impassioned
a lifetime of woe flashing before
my wide permanently-startled orbs

chili beans & jalapenos on my breath,
i screamed that i didn't mean to kill anyone
i only wanted to slay those cruel isms—not a living soul

    (rented myself into a hole,
    yet couldn't afford a grave)

i bit the tit that had nursed me on poison
i then seized my rightful splendor
i not only saw horns, i heard Miles Davis

there were news reports that a swarm of California
quakes had thrown the nation into permanent
recession. there were news reports that poetry
was not dead, just sequestered

my teeth were shards yet i cried his name preceded by an O

feet orbit sleep
thunderheads claw the horizon
sun frozen in azure mounted on stucco
coconut incense & Latin jazz smoke the air
high sensations low thoughts
thunderheads fill the basin
precious objects gather at lips
there is a map of the wind available to chillseekers
spent robins rattle on utility wires
irresolute pieces of sky self-assemble into chevrons & stars
young city blisters cosmos
red spire rises thru thunderheads

the history of rain
is in the fingertips of lovers

i thought i could awaken them myself
my cold sequoia queenfish ritual
a tidal wave of inky torments
rain spit tears urine

distorted light. a distant beacon
reappeared in a feast of bluesy ripples

i offered coffee. i offered brine. i offered sangria

> (i'm anadromous.
> i breathe ocean
> yet actually have
> no proper gills.
> i do not swim because
> i'm of the drowned)

sitnalta

the weather is not an issue
here. nor time.
the rivers concern me
and lakes and reservoirs,
my natural state a wetness

my lover is a land creature made
of stone & bone. he sings to me
of mountains & deserts, boulders, sand

he sings to me the extremes of his earthiness
he sings to me

"come ashore. come ashore and let them sleep."

III

AMERICAN SONNETS (25, 87–100)

today the villains are all named willie
with bushy wild hair which grows heedlessly
spewing discontent/a new breed
of resilient superlice disrespecting all borders
and infesting the puritan scalps
of bloody-handed dealers in cyclopean confusion

each death carried in blank eyes
(they taught us to accept the strangeness
of tolerance) someone discovers a mind
missing for over a decade
making note that all phone messages are from
neglected dunners irate over negligence

this compulsion to write one's name
is a form of post-recession autoeroticism

as we undergo national ustulation

vapor & more vapor
false urgencies & late night prunes
nuthin' but rainy days. how does one save?

"remember," said The Savage, "they only bet on
sure things and the race is fixed"

young & nowhere/old & nowhere
a socio-soviet psyche flayed alive, gored
then gutted
savory but no salvation

a blithering savant's life of frying pans & fires

(let's save the world Negro, but get savvy
there's nothing in it for you but
salvage for the sake & ravishment of others)

managed to get off salvo
failed to veer. vexed at being severed a to vee

looking back. no laugh yet

in this rage of ghostaxis & snuff erotica
can one art rescue another in decline?

(vis-a-vis hydrotherapy & long-term
flood survival: highjack it—one's
only guarantee the ship will dock)

mayday. am trapped in a bag of false positives
on covert travels with self—circling airport
on cruise control. mayday. up to navel
in yellow-bellied lip service. mayday. under
attack by pink pearl erasers

madam. the light at the end of this tunnel
is a streamliner coming head-on

> *bring me*
> *to where*
> *my blood runs*

in pursuit of an avant-garde procedure, the
by-product of a kinky sequence of reflections
announces itself across the chalkboards
of a contentious clan of beef-fed pedants—

holdovers from the days of Conelrad, Thunderbirds
and fizzies with no visible tolerance for
post World War II upstarts or love generation
survivors. tower life is libidinal and disturbed

with fixations on assassinations and bombshells,
bunghole crawling for father figures untarnished
by a savvy revisionism. classrooms filled with
alien darknesses inspire dread and an involuntary

loathing. such cannot be identified with and
invalidates all theories subscribing to mirror-image

between these brown & heavy thighs
boils generations of disgrace
daughter, cruelty could not wear
a more enchanted face—Svengalian & strange

widely widely i open to love. my country
impregnates with seed of hate. conjecture?
no. this mad fornication i endure, jealous
contrary to reason, foolish in my fantasy
that i too am cherished. whose name will the
       bastard verse declaim?

apologize for every sin and kiss my toes

and then, perhaps, my affection
will sear this grave chasmic mouth

o to be dumb again! a virgin smacked in wicked purity

the gates of mercy slammed on the right foot.
they would not permit return and bent
a wing. there was no choice but
to learn to boogaloo. those horrid days
were not without their pleasures, learning
to swear and wearing mock leather so tight
eyes bulged, a stolen puff or two
behind crack-broken backs and tickled palms
in hallways dark, flirtations during choir practice
as the body organized itself against the will
(a mystic gone ballistic, not home but blood
on the range) as one descended on this effed-up
breeding hole of greeds—to suffer chronic seeings

was't hunger or holiness spurred the sighting?

suffering race hysteria and heavy summer,
the purveyors of objectified truths abandon
saintlike discretions in pursuit of tabloid wealth—
introduce a salacious sucking into the vox acus

divert a nation from the death of its individualism
(which, in the absence of any consciousness
certainly cannot be missed) as the stock market soars
and fiction pales beside fact as crimes of perversion
     escalate and

brown-toned babies are sacrificed on concrete slabs.
the strategy is far-reaching, if not obvious, scored in
the impenetrable text of an exclusionary jurisprudence
penned by The Metaphysicians of Dung and endorsed by
intellectual zoo-keepers. the stench raised

panics the tygers, inspires the tramplings of
this temperamental and tormented elephant

when the relationship between head and heart
becomes diseased and disturbed, focus on
the peculiar distends stomachs, shortstops
enthusiasm and bankrupts the covertly emotional

political & cultural life are defined by estrangements

causeless non-viral fevers burn without analgesic
relief, causing skin to peel if not change color.
the strive for parity becomes a death drive, the driven
burned on the pyre of their own fiery idolatries

the ascension of the Joneses to the ritzy heights
of liquor lords, diamond barons and media moguls
voids genuine assessment of the state of our decline
shelving salvageable discourse on the Negro annoyance

hear that beat of Goofy's feet? it's the avenue
he's financed to screw—42nd Street

nostrum nostalgia my notes on never nada no
collect against my reluctance/forced tabulations
dey did dis, say me, and dat and dat dere
why have there been no arrests? no hearings? no justice?
(what is not offered cannot be refused)

i regress/the despoiled child, the deserted schoolyard

weeper. this is your execution
weeper. this is your groveling stone
weeper. yours is the burst & burnings of a city

stunned tearless in the uselessness of limp pursuit
breathlessness besets and brings the ass earthward

rest. the answer yellows and loses its wit, its crispness
my bed to make my heart to stake my soul to take

how i committed suicide: i revealed myself to you.
i trusted you. i forgot the color of my birth

seized by wicked enchantment, i surrendered my song

as i fled for the stars, i saw an earthchild
in a distant hallway, crying out
to his mother, "please don't go away
and leave us." he was, i saw, my son. immediately,
i discontinued my flight

from here, i see the clocktower in a sweep of light,
framed by wild ivy. it pierces all nights to come

i haunt these chambers but they belong to cruel
        churchified insects.
among the books mine go unread, dust-covered.
i write about urban bleeders and breeders, but am
troubled because their tragedies echo mine.

at this moment i am sickened by the urge
to smash. my thighs present themselves

stillborn, misshapened wings within me

clouds descend and obfuscate—vapor evermore

as the city suffers race hysteria & heavy summer
the drive for parity is death by day
and a kinky sequence of reflections presages its birth
twixt heavy brown thighs

inventory begins—swaying bodies converge
a genuine assessment of the decline of our welfare state

you are the languages you speak

(now that the jinn are all uncorked, they waste valuable
wishes worrying the warts over those good ol' days
down bottle, daddy, schmoozing around the hookah—
hopes hopelessly blackened by fruitless efforts to
affect what can't be transformed by magic of any kind)

now that the gates of hell have slammed,
i am seized and surrender my terrible squawk

dark drive down the coast. west then south

i lack the strength to live or the strength to quit
this bloody limbo. ghosts come on the fog with black
eyes eating velvet starlight. i see him pressed against
my body, naked tremblings, hands gripping sheets.

there is nothing to discuss post coitus. there is
no future. there will be no child, merely restless
spinnings in the tender void of whispers. (there
she goes like a sea mother, to deposit her

confusions like eggs in the sand.) sunset begins
another cycle in the struggle to breathe to lust
to find the right combination of words, which will
create the proper whole—*if only to find the mumbojumbo*

dark drive down the coast. dark invigorating drive

intrados. myth-deep in tropical underbelly, he gives
erect hand the grunts the reaching the roar

ageless febrile greediness/endless penetrations

   of her.

the comet blisters the sky yet disintegrates
monoliths crumble with each speaking, the talk
of orchids of rivers of songlessness of cold meat

she reclines on their bed/a catalogue of twistings.
doomed if not addicted, lost if not captured
she knows his hungers. her jade entanglements
      her eyes-to-lips wisdom

that stone hidden in her mouth. rare jass

shaft-deep in she-warmth/those mythic givings (hers)
erect hard his grunts his reach into the abyss, his roar

living with you, he says, *is like living with a Gauguin*

what happened is unclear. doing ninety
in the left lane. heavy breathing in the back seat

it draws blood & saliva. the details unclear

if everything one needs to know according
to the palms. travels with myself/a zany theophany
seeking a permanent pill, (the rock to lean on a rock
upside the head) something to take the stumble
out of this first-fight-then-fuck coranto

uncertain what it means to laugh anymore. rolling
over and over until motionless. clarity
no longer guaranteed. doing ninety

o those so-kissable Judas lips *hotdiggity*

deathscape. *ask for lights & bells & brass rings*

a monster urge to ram the ultimate orange/the
unfamiliar rush/*wings & flames*

doing ninety. skid marks from A to Omaha

when thou dost find no joy in all famed Erato's
honeyed breast, wordsport a gangster poet's jest
how black and luscious comes each double-barreled
phrase, like poisoned roses or a maddened potter's
glaze. words abundant dance their meanings on
a thrilling floor, the stolen song of ravens and
purloined harps galore. this is the gentle game of
maniacs & queens, translations of the highly-souled
into a dreamer's sputterings where dark gives voice
to gazer's light and writerly praise is blessed
incontinence, the spillage of delight. sing to me
thy anthem of untasted fruit. slay in me the
wretchedness that names me brute. liberate my
   half-dead kill. come. glory in my rebirth.
   come. glory in my wonder's will

IV

METAPHYSICALLY NIGGERISH

made slaphappy

 living water   roars   between cauliflower lobes

that night you broke   over my blackness

 and   i found freedom in the roses of your palms

more than saved   there, but wanted   your fingers coaxed

kisses from wind-bruised lips   your coarse fingers

aroused   a smolder   in the cold

your wide treasure-filled heart, eyes intense

oak & amber openings   mysteries

inviting   exploration & greed   we are speaking

now   syllables break   like fine leaded crystal   spill

 emotion/a virgin flow   rich   thick   fragrant

i swear   to you   i have forgotten   what

clocks keep   what the keys fit

where the silence   was   entered

slams the floor
when it enters a room

feels eyeballs bouncing up and down
behind it—left then right

draws hands like magnets

don't need unnecessary support
tingles when properly stroked

can soak in the tub for hours
and the crack still be dirty

can swallow lovers whole
and spit 'em out happy

when Mamaloss survive da middle pass she holler
her dem Scots-Irish troubadour
bring him to her knees
dey get busy copulatin' and conceive the blues

the field and the house are now incorporate
      & incorporeal

      the price of
      justice & equality
      has been raised
      beyond bargaining

jadu hoodoo vudooon wah

"they" will never give up anything
      of true & lasting worth

everahthang costs somebody somewhere at some time
      some unnecessary blood

long-term sweat & heat rashes are internalized
      as sugar, dropsy & soul failure

a mind without genuine social appreciation
      cannot be wasted

the exceptional will be used against the
      unexceptional & those who
are exceptionally unexceptional will be
      criminalized

(what's opted for is maximum profit
      on minimal socioeco investment)

a penchant for the hard does not preclude
a preference for the sweet

we always collect our firsts

three rooms and a jane

this dust-congested firetrap is too small
the bedroom is a boulevard, the bathroom
a battlefield. layers of iron-tainted pain eel
from cracked and crumbling plaster. we're too big
for it, our rhythms stain and strain ancient pipes
and broken tile. there's no room to move.
privacy is shared with four-inch-long Japanese
night crawlers who squirm in on our thoughts
like secrets/like the notes mangled by the Armenian kid
practicing violin one floor below, or the moans
of the Mexican bride to the salsa of her
husband's fists, one wall over—a tarantula for nosey
neighbors. the odor of mold oozes from beneath
the staircase of splinters, to mingle with
globules of grease dotting the air, gumming
up the white plastic window shades concealing
naked pleadings for mothering and
children children please keep down the need
mama is trying
(to be sung to the rustle of Hollywood rats)
there's plenty of room for work, too much for worry
but no room to lay down, no place to sit
and soak, relaxation as much a joke
as separate-but-equal. we're too big for it,
bloated. our rages cramped and swollen,
on the ever-stinking brink

three rooms and a jane

i make my faithful dead saccharin promises
on the oceanside afternoons of summer,
tell them iced-tea stories, my lips numb
from bumping the air during fast talk, my head
reeling with the skeletons of episodes/a tombload
of urgencies—each jealous of the others
all as impatient with me as ever

i'm boxed in, foil wrapped by
brutal expectations & the demise of industry
i confess i'm sorry to disappoint them

they complain, those loving hants, because
i offer them cookies as if they were guests.
they demand to know when does it get down to
the collards & pepper-fried steak
(they're anxious to get their napkins dirty)
"soul food," i protest,
"is too heavy, this climate considered"
and i justify this by explaining
it will sit on their consciousness for hours

how then, they moan, will we ever breathe again?

and when i fail to answer, they slam their plates
against the stone

take better care of your business, they warn,
or you will soon join us

no. i am not a liar
(that's one of the phrases i'm quick to repeat)
it's an unusual matter, a combination of

night blindness and day stroke
complicated by compulsions for neatness
and costume jewelry

"look," i say, "after all, it's not my fault
that i'm divided against myself—
half homemaker, half renegade bitch.
i'm a post V-J Day schizophrenic,
a madness from which there's no recovery."

bullcocka (believe me, the dead can swear
as colorfully as the living)

they stare back at me,
gingerly brush away the crumbs
and after a prolonged silence,
icily request cold beer at the next sitting

when in a mellow zone
i think of your sad cheap pale yellow coffin
how it hurt to tell our folk
not to put what little you could scrimp into
    the ground
how i am separated from you
by twelve years and an eternity
still condemned to stew on this side
of the window pane
looking in at the calm, envying the events
others enjoy/are part of

guess what i see. you know, certainly

the Marina boats
with their fine sleeknesses and Mondrian spars
anchored off a foreign blueness
i stare at from behind chain links and razor wire

just now
our pale yellow sedan gleams in the rented
driveway. we've named it El Sid (Jewish, sort of)
we're flat busted, he and i, and in debt to three government
agencies, four megacorporations, four old
friends and two new friends. i've been up working
& thinking after writing in my sleep all night

sweating money & sunshine & how

just then i envisioned
you, darting out of the manicured bushes
secluding the Santa Monica Yacht Club
screaming at the blonde-skinned swells in Picasso

print sundresses, screaming that trendy charity
funds aren't enough, that tax deductions for
failures aren't enough, that ruinous divorce
settlements, cultural tourism, acupuncture
and antidepressants are not enough, and go eff
your sadomasochistic applause

and i remembered the last time we spoke.
you whispered the secret of your fame: hustle
that fine brown behind
and take what's for the shaking before it sags

and i admired your guts if not your limited vocabulary

wondering
how many of those frosty bitches we could've
neutralized, the two of us, had we fought side-by-side
throwing blows & bricks, rioting coast-to-coast
burning & looting from Harlem to Hollywood Park

today you're toes-up in the dust factory
a hit & split, struck down by cancer at sunrise
dig that cloaked surgeon at the wheel
the car spins the brakes lock the rubber burns!
in one drunken wheee you're knocked sky high
and only your fatness falls back to earth

(or was that What-Was-Her-Name lurking in the twilit
        shadows?)

and you
have become a redundancy—a spook now a spook
unceremoniously exposed in post-chemo
convulsions clawing fluid-stained sheets,
gasping at oblivion
more real at last than those public deaths
you were so fond of staging

(you forgave them all once but won't forgive this dying)

i didn't have time to watch you
hurry through this world. i was too
busy hurrying along myself. i did catch
a glimpse of you, once, doped up & nodding
on the romance of rhetoric & poetic diction
stoned out of your ego on a hard-earned
cocktail of bombast & youthful adulation

we belonged to the same cult, you & i, they tell me
that gathering of smoke-colored women
who rise and take shape against the evil logic
of a virulent hate
the unrepentant women with strong loves & stronger woes
the women accused of & found guilty of
taking their spare lives too seriously, the women
who rudely refuse to bend for the soulfuck

the women who live on the astonished wind

were i the queen of sleight of hand
i'd steal the wind from a thunderstorm
    if i could
i'd steal the sweetness out of fresh-baked bread
    it smells so good
i'd steal the stink from the core of night
i'd steal the thrill in a thief's delight
    know i would
    steal the wings off the flitting dove
    the memory
    of a brother's love
i'd steal the t from the end of time
i'd steal the wolf of a nursery rhyme
i'd steal the dither from its troubled spin
i'd steal my mind from the brain its in
i'd steal the rose from the end of bloom
i'd steal my son from his cancer's doom
i'd steal the corners from my frown
i'd steal your smile if it wasn't nailed down
were i the queen of sleight of hand
i'd steal the poison from this muthaland

> *When the monkeys are on stage, no one*
> *notices a death in the house.*
>
> —*Hollywood Proverb*

poisoned brains, scrambled thoughts & gravy/
    identification
without charm. no restitution made and anything that
    calls itself Black
is shunted to the back pages or in with the loonies
    the journey
toward ongoing reward derailed. in a maddening series
    of calculated
accidents the accumulated debt blows away all
    possibilities.
voice & vision vanish in hard unfinished splendor.
    a certain number
of numbered citizens sacrificed for the ultimate gobble.
    (she is bored in
Burbank but can't get work anywhere else.) high
    culture has been
exterminated in the name of exclusion of Black Rage
    and (gasp) payback.
everyone has gone lala/has become shakers of money-
    makers.
    culture, like God,
is dadblasted with no hope for resurrection, resurgence
    or regurgitation
and no reparations (call it juice money). she's goose—off
    the integrationist
A-list/just another nobody too smart for her own dark.
    everybody who
is nobody is at the symposium for dunces on the
    rudimentary
elements of pretentious abstraction in late

20th Century
America where the real crankmasters do all the hard
        poopoo while
the posers collect the checks as the new expatriates
        religiously exploit
domestic racism rising to the top of the ivy-tower
        wage system
without really sucking or having pubic hairs singed

   the cultural tourists cloak
   themselves in our violence, come
   begging authenticity, come to bask in
   the sun of our rages. they offer us
   their dexter hands and cross the fingers
   on their sinister hands. they write
   plays about our violence. they
   roast meat on the spit of our rages.
   they profit off the bricks & bottles
   thrown thru plate-glass complacency.
   they offer us true words from the podium
   but pen White lies for the press.
   they absolve the guilty. they warm
   their butts by our fires of outrage.
   they take our blood to the bank

(since experiences other than electronic transfer
        and networking are
no longer of value particularly when not waxing inanely
        and forever about
the connections between man and nature as if cities
        are not by-products
of a dissatisfaction with precisely what's found untamed/
        precisely what bites,
like sole-eating viruses (imparting new meaning to
        loose shoes), as if
something has been lost as opposed to overlooked or

deliberately omitted).
there's no time at all for the retrograde babblings
of dispossessed
doomsayers docked benefits, who cannot be seen
from the heights
of corporate cloisters or within the cozy confines
of concord jets or
while hanging from vines of billionaires (say it again,
Sambolina—a miss
is still a miss). a certain penchant for dropping French
phrases and names
of jazz heroes remains voguish and has literary value
as does being descended
from foreign royalty or deposed dictators or robber
barons (just now
there is nothing to it, the racings of the brain
as in certain visual
stimulation generating salivation, lubrication and emission)
and/or to the extent
that one generates such arousal—determining behavior
in closed environments.
uh—discourse on the size and quality of the buzz tabled
until there are
enough looters present to make a respectable quorum
o hickory dickery

darn things get a mite boogerish

lacking realization. dreams are apt to sour
to get bloodshot & baggy-eyed.
they'll stop shaving and neglect their teeth.
they won't go near a shower,
and their feet & armpits will start stinking
up the place, dirt collecting under unclipped nails

they'll quit going to church on Sundays

they'll snore bare funky ass-up
till noon, eat candy bars & drink beer
for breakfast, sit around the house half-dressed
in old blue jeans and raggedy sneakers, smoke
a cancer a day and stew over sleaze magazines
until sunset, crawl the neighborhood
in tore-down coupes after dark, scoping for
trouble. they'll come in drunk or monkeyed up (both)

and slap around the smart ideas

when dreams go bad
they're apt to get mean,
foul-mouthed. violent.

they're apt to turn killer

ugly bird in solitary flight
whose nesting place will you steal tonight?

sorrow travels light travels fast travels
alone. her father's gray eyes her mother's
hurtful touch. a shrouded figure. from funeral
to funeral. begging memories, scavenging ghosts,
rooting up praise. gone along now. fingering
the heartcloth. scrapes ashes from the pyre of
her harpy tongue. Atones

ugly peahen doing a solo wingflap west
some birdbrain told you you could fly

slavery was indeed hard. living is precondition
for dying. spinning tops stop spinning. Picasso
could draw. chitterlings are delicious when
properly cleaned and cooked right

cross-eyed cornflake-yellow auspex of urban blather

barren/without decency's spark
the only child you give birth to
is yourself and you squat to lay it
like an egg—out the wrong hole

—for D.L.L., N.G., Trudier &
the booster

i don't love you because

there's no magic in the poverty
you fatten on and then break wind in public
and because you have the unmitigated grit
of the progressively impaired

earth will eventually fall into the sun. news?
mere example of your unoriginal scarfings.
you speak simplistically of complex things
you are a part of the unnatural order of our nation

like cigar smoke in a locked broom closet
like a thin cotton coat in subzero weather
like redolent zits on the blue face

i do not love you because

there is no music in either your soul
or your Africanized Negro buffoonery.
you're as weighty as butterfly shit

you have squandered the attention of academic idiots
and idiots in general. they applaud you—
the shadow malignancy that also exploits our race

you have made black a dirty word. again

the word never got out, not then—
not now. it was half jive if
not all jive. the unborn hero was
born to never live to be a man.
he was molested & murdered every day
of the week. it was half jive if
not all. no one hip to his shit was
able to do squat about it. and those
who could do diddly were preoccupied
with floor-showing & high-signing.
it was half jive if not all. the
wall endured but the nappy head was
broken. the hearts & souls of lesser
men were not stirred. the world knows
not to call here because the phone
is disconnected. it was mainly jive.
besides they had something wicked for
his uppity ebony behind even Einstein
could not anticipate. it was damned
near all jive. the bright eye of
the believer was stabbed blind,
the scrotum was abscessed before
it was yanked out with pliers, and
a cocaine-induced stroke has given
the New Messiah a permanent grin
to worry about. it was much too much
if not all jive. history maliciously
repeated, the moment missed when
John Wayne ceased being an actor and
became an economic philosophy. if they
were dead then they are really dead
now. it was the jive of the century.
and all the Malcolms left are buying
lunch and burial plans on bad credit

dear cousin DJ,

it doesn't take a degree in particle physics
to understand social injustice

thirty years of schmoozing over a chessboard,
empty rhetoric and chasing pussy has not improved
your posture and
all that elder statesman bourgeois
you spew to the naïfs sounds simply old.
in your last incarnation you were pootbutt. in
this one, you are merely a poot

what you carry between your thighs is
not a sacred truth, but an integrity so minute
it can't even be detected with a magnifying glass

you're so retrograde you don't know
that Master Communicator is a euphemism for
just-another-goddamned liar

shaky

your head is on ass-backwards and
all the power you possess wouldn't jump start a gnat

you're so okey-doke even your boogers are contrived

can you say L-A-Z-Y?

your thick blazing lips are ever wrapped
around words so full of black fire they singe
unprotected ears. but your illegitimate

children are not only bluster-deaf, they're
bookless & freezing, cry rage-colored tears
and still toddle around in diddies (which looks
strange now that they have pubic hair)

how dare you complain that "little has changed"—
because in your cowardice you have not changed it

your words smolder but your hands are cold & spotless.
you have never touched a brick a gun or a shovel.

and you cling to your imaginary glory like a fungus

she put the whammy
    on you
she say you a bald-headed
    back stabber
she put the whammy on you
    she say you
nevah rise above your
    eyeballs
she put the whammy
    on you. she
say your baby soul still doo-doo
    in diapers
she put the whammy on you
    she say
your kidneys are made of cheese
    she put
the whammy on you. she say
    when you
dead nuthin' happen
    cuz you
don't rate a ghost

—after the song by Herbie Hancock

ghostlovers those old urges in furious forward
tongue & veiny hard-ons/stingers strokers
stumblebums—thunderjolts & madhens—all decisions

are wrong. two-thirds stomach/a will of its own.
pick a month, like January. lay out the days
a crazed calendar, a snowless chill. bad wind

you say? buzz it. oxygen-starved lungs which
have become scream-weakened. never-ending list
of rip-offs. it's all fuckdaddies & parasites

roiling in the gutbucket/like breaded and fried
deep dish in Rex lard/a river of fat in which
gizzards, hushpuppies and thoughts are browned,

eyes wide as magnolia blossoms, limbs askew but
sinewy and glutted on touch *dem thigh bones*
potlikker laced with spit & Johnny Walker black,

ham-hock-sprouting mid bowl in butter beans.
you know you're just a greedy so-and-so
working chain rhymes, stringing nostrums like beads

you say chapter & verse, "this is the way they do
it to you here." zzzt. that which doesn't sting
you stupid makes you cynical/bugged. but for the

light of it all, mean things winging in the green,
the swelling comes heavy, calm stifled in folds
of irritated jones-maddened meat. a dull buzz to the

quick then the marrow, capillaries bursting like
star orchids, an itchless rash webbing the skin
as if an acid burn, scars puffed at full rise

as big as confessions of attempted excellence.
roundness rages, bones in retreat, order rules on
its own as the abyss sets behind voluminous cheeks

major bloat signals the decline in bull to shoot—soft
tissue damage. cash cows belly up in lost focus, as you
practice the science of floating in one's own waste.

i saw a squad car pull up outside
the grocery store as i was
leaving it. i had just bought a pack
of Big Red Gum and some Zig-Zag
rolling papers. i knew they'd take
one look at me and stop me.
i lived in the neighborhood and all i
needed was the embarrassment
of being patted down in front of every
toothy snot-nosed nubbin-headed gossip-
monger for blocks. i wanted to vomit.
here i come walking out of the store with
nothing but my purse, scantily dressed
because it's 96° in the skimpy shade
and these grinning donut holes are
gonna jack me up right here on the
goddamned street just so my palms
can fry on the hood of their Crown Vic

the operating stereotype that
i'm a working girl instead of a woman
who works for her living—the gum
is for a friend, the papers purchased
at my about-to-be ex-husband's request

there go all my plans for later

they began stepping out of their ride
the way authority steps.
i was about to make their morning
if not the entire day.
i had important business,
my fake attitude said. yeah, we

can guess, said their salacious sham
smiles. i began walking toward
the bus stop pretending like i had
intended to do so all along.
my heart was jitterbugging
against my scalp. "o miss, we'd like
to have a word." i pretended to
look for a bus, to be impatient. and
then i looked at them. "you! come
over here," ordered the pretty
one. "we've got something hanging
for your big ugly black ass"

it makes me nervous to go into a store
because i never know if i'm going to
come out. have you noticed how much
they look like prisons these days? no display
windows anymore. all that cold soulless
lighting—as atmospheric as county jail—
and all that ground-breaking status-quo
shattering rock 'n' roll reduced to neuron
pablum and piped in over the escalators.
breaks my rebel heart. and i especially
hate the aroma of fresh-nuked popcorn
rushing my nose, throwing my stomach
off balance. eyes follow me everywhere
like i'm a neon sign that shouts shoplifter.
and so many snide counter rats want to
service me, it almost makes me feel rich
and royal. that's why i rarely bother to
browse. i go straight to the department
of object of conjecture, make my decision
quick, throw down the cash and split

one time i had barely left this store
when i heard somebody yelling stop! stop!
i turned around and this dough-fleshed
armed security guard was waving me down.
i waited while he caught his breath and
demanded to search my purse i stared him
into his socks. we're outside the store,
i reminded him. if you search me, you'd
better find some goddamned something.
he took a minute to examine my eyes, turned
around and went back to his job, snorting
dust and coondogging teenage loiterers

you saw me when i came in, drawn
by your fire sale sign

i have entered your shop
to spend my slave's wages on goods
you pretend are available to anyone

i have behaved like a lady
joined the line and have stood here forever
without complaining even though
my feet are screaming and i'm suffering
from a raging heartache

and now it is my turn
to opt for what i want. and you suddenly
do not see me. even though
i'm as black as blazes as tall
as a drink of salt water and wide as two stadiums
even though
i am standing within stabbing distance

your eyes see everything around me but me

and then you look straight at the White
person behind me, lean forward
and ask, "may i help you?"

at least they have sense enough to squirm
before i clear my throat

this is the last LIQ on the edge
of reality. a not-so-old woman trembles
behind the counter, her tiny yellow feet
swallowed in working clogs,
her smock and slacks bag over her dry
fleshlessness in the way
her husband sees her when he beats her
because she stands between
him and a fool's fantasy, or what her
arrogant neo-American son
sees when he tells mom he doesn't
have to listen to her
anymore or what the buyer sees,
towering over her in the ill-lit gloom,
that peering resentful silence
weighs every move in fright & anger.
she's so tiny. what a place
to be killed in, dying with the
daily anticipation of robbery & murder
at the hands of juvenile robbers/
young bloods indifferent to
the lifelong trauma that radiates
from below those twitchy lashes
in that crypt the color of grapefruit

here

in the liquor store at the butt end of time
her hands claw the cash register for change
lays it on the counter
gentle as quail eggs. no smile
today. struck yellow. nothing to say.
a simple turn of the head, enough

to confirm the customer has
vanished. the transaction completed.
maybe she'll survive this
eternity on her feet

here

at the devil's liquor locker
the sum of her ignorance greater
than the niggling parts/she counts her bank
mentally. it helps pass the hours
without adequate help or refreshment, the
constant inventory of a cultural
loneliness. she's one plane flight away
from the familiar, stuck in these afternoons
filled with the unsuspecting laughter
of black school children who swarm
the shelves to spend their allowances on
sugar and salt, or to pocket as much
as they can conceal, sometimes dashing
out the door, sometimes calling
her ugly names, sometimes speaking to
her silence as if it were a parent or
a teacher or a cop. ma'am,
how much do this cost? and she is
numbstruck by their boldness, how they
playfully or contemptuously read
her foreign mood how they understand
the physics of mean looks
how those brown eyes read
her loathing even as she takes their cash
how all that is African stares into
her bleakness and understands
a soul devoid of song

i was shopping for a new nightie
in this shopping mall. there was this
place called the unique boutique
all smoke-tinted glass & retro 60s chic
and this henna-job simpleton comes
up and parks her stroller-bound brat
right at my heels and walks off
like i'm instant baby-sitter. i look
down at the child and catch those
enormous blue eyes like flies in a cup.
her or his head is a slur of red just
like mama's and i don't dare move
for sweating. sure enough. i can tell
i'm being sized-up. to dread or not
dread. what IS it? and then the tot's
head starts to spin and its mouth opens
like a siren and the whole damned
joint is in a sudden panic about
this molester in mammy's clothing

babychile, now that you've matured

beyond age eighteen and they haven't
killed you, the next step? butt plucking

snatched
from the arms of mother father community you
are to be stripped of street clothes and
personhood, placed first in cuffs, then state
custody. deloused and deloved

fingerprinted, mug shot, numbered

uniformed
our shame, you will be uniformly shunted in with
the thousands who were once our future our army our
humanity our salvation our joy

now jes' mo canned niggah

no shank. not even a butter knife
no glass and human contact limited by grace
of the warders. food will arrive via voiceless robot
in portions measured to keep the body—minimally
you will dine with plastic utensils
and wheeze about second helpings being legend

no weights to lift. no worthwhile books
to read. and god knows no basketball
on the yard. valueless predigested
TV and the pap of mainstream movies
for the grist of philosophy and psychology

139

your mind must die like it's supposed to

in the new scientifically sterile slams
where no dust settles and there
are no birds or vermin for pets. inmates
packed in so solitarily consensual sex of any
kind is unheard of in this dimness without dark,
a lens spying into every orifice
the tongues the breasts the genitals massaged
by hand will be on view for the amusement
of those jivekeepers unless you're too shy
        to masturbate on camera

trapped in the prison of recriminations
sputtering to the broke syntax of imaginary crime
you will rat yourself out daily
to those invisible keepers who declared you
incorrigible at your moment of conception
yes. i did it. i was black. and thus-and-so

but now you're canned sorry nothing niggah

packed in maximum isolation
sockets but no eyes to see
spine bone as soft as pink as salmon
hermetically sealed and salt free

fungi are holding union meetings in
    your urine-stained
mattress. music is the uneven shuffle
    of mules along
slate-gray corridors, followed by
    the pause that
listens to mice munch in the walls
    speaking frankly
has earned you retirement in neutral
    and a squat
on the sun deck slumped & soap-witted
    in a cushionless
white plastic patio chair, the drool
    on your chin
and vomit on your eyeglasses have
    caked solid,
sunbaked, while your new but unwanted
    tan fails to
conceal liver spots & verrucae. all the
    living you've
hoarded adds up to neglect fostered by
    staff cuts and
unmonitored dosages of awareness-killers.
    the numbness and
tingling between your thighs is the
    result of an
indifferent nursing attendant's failure
    to do her job,
the proper bathing, as is the weeping
    abdominal rash
hidden by your thrift-shop kimono.
    the voices you
hear tearing around in your head

are those of a
young woman and her lover arguing over
    the wisdom of
bringing children into their bleak
    inner-city realm.
you awaken from your nap to find you
    are still napping
and are startled when the lizards in your lap
    jump toward
your chin and you recognize your tits

you are a foreigner here. this is my skin.
it is made of wild Santa Anas raging through canyons
and is as thin as a saint's aura.
i wear the night in my hair, stars glistening there
like rhinestones in a net of back silken naps.
the heat that cracks and dries your consciousness
is my breath on my lover's chest. you have no claim here.
there is nothing for you to wax romantic about.
you know nothing. you've invested nothing.
heart sacrifice is the only sacrifice.
lean into the blade, if you're so brave.
no one survives here who still has a reason

1

jes another X marking it

dangling gold chains & pinky rings
nineteen. done in black leather & defiance
teeth white as halogen lamps, skin dark as a threat

they spotted him taking in the night
made for the roust
arrested him on "suspicion of"
they say he became violent
they say he became combative in the rear seat of
that sleek zebra maria. they say
it took a chokehold to restrain him
and then they say he died of asphyxiation
on the spot

summarized in the coroner's report
as the demise of one
more nondescript dustbunny
ripped on phencyclidine
(which justified their need to
leave his hands cuffed behind his back
long after rigor mortis set in)

2

stress had damaged his thirty-nine-year-old mind
more than he could admit but he was trying
to make life work as well as it could
for a father with three children praying
dad will pull through

where the butcher knife came from
no one's sure. they say
he held off ten riot squad patrol cars
for forty-five minutes outside that 109th Street
church. they say the cops had stopped him
because they didn't like his looks.
they say something fragile inside his head
snapped. they say it took twenty rounds of ammo
to bring him down they say he took five
gunshot pellets & thirteen bullets
they say that was a lot of outrage over
a case of misconstrued identity

3

she was fed up that day with
everything. now here they come turning off
the damned gas so she went and
chased the service rep
from the yard before he could carry out the
disconnection order. by the time
police officers arrived she had lost what was
left of her common sense
had grabbed up & brandished an eleven-inch
boning knife to back up her mouth.
the two officers complained she threw
that knife at them. and they were so terrified
they didn't consider a wounding. they
simply emptied both guns into
the thirty-nine-year-old hefty female.
it took twelve shots to
subdue all that treataniggahthis
and whitesonofabitchesthat,
they said, and kill it

strangely he was dodging & ducking,
    bouncing & rolling,
    tipping & slipping
(as if dangling from the end of it)
in and out of traffic in front of the sheriff's
station, embarrassing them, causing a modest jam
    for no apparent reason
therefore they arrested the twenty-six-year-old
descendant of slaves and booked him for
this queer behavior, their spokesman said
    because there weren't
enough terrorists, assassins or irate taxpayers
to keep them busy that Wednesday afternoon.
    he was handcuffed
and left alone in his cell and fell inexplicably
into unconsciousness in a mere three hours,
    they said. he was
rushed to a nearby hospital still in cuffs
where he died within twenty-two minutes

cause of demise as unknown as ever

without evidence to support the supposition
they swore the twenty-one-year-old
consumer was involved in the robbery of the
popular Manchester Avenue chicken shack,
and not just another hungry-but-innocent bystander
he was assumed guilty, if not the brainiac
perhaps the getaway driver. he was captured during
the fray before questions could be asked or
players & slayers identified. that he was unarmed
was not a pertinent issue. that he was ignorant

decidedly was. they handcuffed him and made
him lay on the ground in the middle of the fray
where, unfortunately, his ignorance got
him killed by police gunfire. they say an officer
yelled freeze and this inexperienced
young black hoodlum being unfamiliar with the
procedure of how one freezes while being held face down
on the sidewalk, hands cuffed behind one's back
could not do so. therefore the inability to freeze
under these conditions cost him his life

6

exhausted after working the nightshift
he was so dead on his feet he couldn't
hear 'em ramming in his door, so they broke into
the sepia-toned man's apartment by mistake
(it was supposed to be the one downstairs).
officers swarmed his bed as he opened his eyes,
officers were on him like maggots on foul meat.
nevertheless he managed to free himself long
enough to run into the bathroom where
he was ultimately subdued without ever knowing why

the coroner reported this
as death due to heart attack
brought on by advanced arteriosclerosis
in a twenty-eight-year-old black male

7

he was bound for college but was caught
standing on a street corner blocks from home
maybe, like they say, he had recently scored some
dope (which could not be found) or maybe
minutes earlier he'd been snacking on that ham

sandwich mama made for her nineteen-year-old
sure is handsome fine young black man.
maybe there was nothing to it at all, not even
that missing piece of aluminum foil the officers
claim they saw him pull out of his trousers

sudden-like

as they happened to be cruising past. it made
a mysterious metallic gleam

which they mistook for the glint of steel
which is why there was all that draw-and-fire
which is why

mama went to his funeral instead of his graduation

8

all of twenty-six, the ebony diabetic had
no steady job and lived with his parents.
he was a young man with mental & physical
problems. he began to act strangely, they say
although no one noticed him brandishing
that piece of radiator fan belt or that
kitchen knife in the middle of the street.
perhaps some car somewhere had broken down
certainly, he had, enough to make the sheriff's
deputies approach with caution and order him
to freeze. he turned toward them and even
though he was fourteen feet away from them his
turning toward them inspired so much fear
in the armed men one of them emptied his
Smith & Wesson service revolver into the
young diabetic who died from three slugs

9

that night Bob came blamming on her door.
she had just gotten home from working
the register at the club and her feet were
killing her, now here come some numbskull
sayhisnameis Bob knocking the damn door
in with some okey-doke about "here come da
police. hide me quick!" so she got something
for Bob's jive probably-drunk ass, that .22
caliber rifle she uses regularly to scare off
the riffraff. then she cracked the door a taste
but before she could make her melodrama move
it slammed open and she was blinded by the
flash as she took a shot in her left breast.
the bullet entered her right rib cage and killed
the 8½-month-old baby she was carrying.
all this behind a supposedtobe drug bust where
no drugs were found by the officers in charge

jes another X marking it

—for C. Jerome Woods

what we do doesn't come up to anybody's standards
not even our own
but we know we have no choice
but to keep on doing

what we do out of grief sadness depression
what our grandmothers & mothers did

what we apologize for
and what we refuse to apologize for
when the responsibility is not ours

what it is (a mischievous inversion of a phrase
frequently spoken impatiently
by a "superior" who is annoyed at having
their leisure interrupted to address
The Problem)

what we know to our souls
is a raw deal. the joke of this journey.
the faster we walk
the longer the road becomes

four centuries of do & done did

what we owe humanity
is what we owe our living children
our dead kith & kin, the unborn
and ourselves

what they refuse to allow us to speak
openly about

no matter how many articulate spokesfolk
we pop out of the universities

yes. what we do isn't always the best
under the givens but if what we do profoundly
threatens to uproot the wrong done us
you can betcha-by-googoo-wow, sweetmeat
the doer will be done in

what some of us have worn out our knees
praying for
what others have worn out our hearts
laboring for
what a few picked up the gun and
went out to get

what need not be spelled out
to anyone too pig-headed to understand
exactly what is meant

what we do. what we have always done

at nightfall he takes his old kerosene
lamp and goes out. if i ask him where
he's going he says to see what he can get

into. he always comes in about cockcrow.
sometimes there's a sweat to him
and the sweet smell of earth. sometimes

he's wild-eyed and walks past me without
a word. if he looks at me it's thru me
to the beyond. sometimes he comes in, says

he's hungry and asks me to rustle up
breakfast. eggs always, sausage usually
and hot biscuits light & fluffy with

goo-gobs of deep brown apple butter. he
downs it with buttermilk or clabber.
we live in the house by the railroad

tracks where the freight don't run no
more. weeds and stones and gravel
everywhere. there's a big ol' peach tree

in the yard that grows sweet orangy-meat
elbertas the size of baseballs. our house
is the one made of wood and got a cracked

shingled roof. it don't look like much
but it's sturdy. the double clothesline
runs along the little patch of yard we

got out back. sometimes the starlings
perch there for a moment. once in a while
a few pigeons come nest in the eaves

i hear 'em cooing like hungry spirits
at a feed. it's his house. he brung me
here to be his woman and see to his needs.

he showed up one day at the house
dressed in his Sunday best. my parents
scared of him but didn't object. they let

him come in. it was strange. almost like
he cast a spell and they were under it.
he stood so tall his fedora hat near

touched the ceiling. he spoke in a warm
deep-velvet voice, asked my daddy for me.
said he'd heard they had a daughter so

black and ugly no man want her. my
parents got a look on they face but
didn't answer his question exactly

except to say, she's our'n and we love
her. i know it ain't the custom, he said,
but if she consents to be my wife i'll give

you thirty golden eagles. my father's eyes
lit up when he saw the gold coins. my
great granddad left 'em to me, he smiled.

my parents looked over into the corner
where i was hiding in the shadows.
i stepped forward and nodded. i knew how

bad they needed the money and it made me
feel proud any man would want me enough
to part with his inheritance. i knew i

could be good to him. i knew i'd make him
appreciate me. he would like my fine neat
stitchin' and embroidery. the perfect way

i could starch and iron a white dress shirt.
the way i could make a bed so taut a quarter
would bounce in its middle the way i could

catch dust before it had time to settle
the way i could bake a two-layer cake
so tall & light it was like eatin' a sweet

cloud the way i could calm a fever and
concoct a remedy the way i could quote
the scriptures as if i'd written the text

the way i could hum songs like a choir
of honey-fat bees. we stood before the preacher
then he carried me home here. the house is

quiet today with just me cleaning, humming,
doing my doings. the floors are swept clean
and waxed. the walls and cabinets are spotless.

yet there's

a fragrance here. it's him. he fills the air like ...

inside a bank vault atop
    a bed of unbound money, paper & coins
        until our heat makes the ink run and the metal flow

    bath soaps and shoe polish
    shaving cremes and lotions
    sweet gum and cigarettes
    his god-given stink

a man's neck is his best feature, the way it slopes and
    lengthens into the curve of his back, shoulders
        and chest. then his upper thighs
            as points of prowess go

in his parents' bed where he was napping after
    our long drive north and on waking, appetite
        restored and erect, he pulled me into my shame

    perhaps music
        perhaps smoke
            perhaps darkness
                perhaps a place either soft or hard

    (when it moves, move with it. duck, cover and hold.)

what comes thru naturally is enough

against the floor, penetration is deeper and more intense
    bones and flesh vibrate and may burn carpet

hair? who cares

one-on-one is best. appreciation

deepens with time in knowing & revelations
   anxieties give way to a trusting tongue
      sharing film noir and fundamental truths

my mind is my biggest organ. brain power the best turn-on

     (having him is nearly daily sometimes
     more than once, mainly afternoons and
     mornings even when my moon comes down
     on me. i do not know who is escaping
     into whom. frequently, i feel him all
     over me like a second blackness.)

    i put my mouth there
  he puts his mouth there
we put our mouths there

body means nothing. self-confidence is the buzz
   followed by a fearless caress

   hot and spicy appetizers
   washed down with sangria or
   tequila, neat—no lime no salt

enjoyed twilight by music or at sunrise
blues wanes or Bartok segues into a lover's drowse

restlessness comes on the muted sounds of
   late night street traffic, excitement aroused
     in the aftermath of the carnal expressed. comes
the wanting. to go out into a cool strangeness
   where i am the danger

Tanya put the wineglass down.
    She can't find it.
She look everywhere. She look all over
the master bedroom, on the night stand,
    on the dresser
near the jewelry box. She look in the master
bathroom across the sink strewn with cups
    holding various
things, assorted tooth brushes, razors,
hairpins, incense and old bits of soap.
    It not there. She
look in the kitchen, then laundry room.
They spick and span. No wineglass.
    She can't remember
if she drank all the wine or not. She wants
a little more. What'd she do with
    that damned glass?
She look in the living room. It ain't there.
The TV float up in her face. All those
    pretty people smiling.
She wish she could smile like that. She
push the TV away and it settles back in
    its place. She search
the cluttered dining room table. It not there.
This bad magazine flaps its pages in her face.
    She hate the wind.
It smells like bowel movement. She slaps the
magazine and it skids off the table onto
    the floor. Where that
glass of wine go? This is making her very upset.
    Tanya she start to cry.
She can't never find nuthin'. She spend the
whole day long searching. It keeps her

from ever going out.
How she gonna ever enjoy the world when
      she spend all her time
      looking for one thing
or another. Where that wineglass up and go?

She hear a ring like crystal. And then the red
      come rushing.

after a night of double nut fudge
expect the end to arrive that morning

you will be burnt face up
turned over and burnt on the backside

you will become blacker by the minute
as your vagueness becomes distinct
and you realize you have ceased to have
value no matter how strongly you've pledged
        your allegiance

New Riddle of the Sphinx: What do you beget
if you cross immortal peaches with drinking gourds?

after decades of shoveling
the spoon will weigh two tons
lifting it will herniate a disc, bring on
sciatica, and put a hurtin' on the core organ

beware of kalimba players with loose thumbs
and polished nails

regarding bad fruit: the deeper the hunger
the sweeter the worm

glimmerings of castrated history emerge from
a buried world thought lost
pried open by the swell & bloat of time
magnanimity in grace of psyche & soma
as within the groin spirits arise/darkest dark
    strong mahogany wood
bursts of ancient stirrings
the release into firmament of the vortex named soul
    gives back the sun
the armies of eternity bleed dry all flags
(*Christian, free, English,* still they say)
the hunger hidden in the tome erupts and
    cracks the silent gray
a sweet death flows as secrets rain
and Africa rules Olympus

V

RETRO ROGUE ANTHOLOGY

—*after A.R. Ammons*

'Tis a far far drive to my digs
come there by a cruisin' car,
sweat in the sun and peer
at outcroppings of rock.
Lizards dart in the brush.

Talk to the wind and tumble-
weed. Or hire a limousine
so the heat doesn't bake
your brain as hard as California clay
or glaze your thoughts.

Ask the chauffeur for
music, Stravinsky or Lotte Lenya
Bootsy or Marvin Gaye—mellow
back and sip the brandy from his flask
thumb through a book of dreams

for a suitable gift. If you leave
at midnight you'll arrive at
midnight, so take it one noon at a time
and I will greet you with
a pitcher of cool pink lemonade.

Swap stories with the driver
about the old days when it was
good and you were bad and lick
the luck that keeps you living long
enough to embellish the tale.

Have him take the first turn
at the tip of the crescent and ride the map

of love's cascade where jacarandas shed,
    the air is salty sultry,
        and it's July all year round.

        Come west of west to my digs, sit
    down and put up your feet.
I've found old rhythms to new blues.
    There's a fresh slab on the coals
        and layer cake a full hand deep.

—after Alan Ansen

1. No need to highjack an airplane. What you're looking
    for is right here under your dirty hypocritical nose.
    And if starved, far from simple.

2. Adoration may be a tall titty, but there's plenty that's
    steatopygous & beautiful right here—enough to soothe
    your corpulent ego for years.

3. You gots hot hands, Krupa. Fry that fat.

—after John Ashbery

No charges of treason—yet—so the property
remains untouched if not untaxed.
And surely bigger banks and asses have been broken
in half or into, making for happy thieves.
Timeless hands have made valueless change.
(Honey, here you are with a toothpick
when what's required is a meat cleaver.)
The TV trays are all set up, dinner's in the oven,
there's raspberry trifle for dessert.
A robe awaits wearer, hangs limp and ill-formed,
gathers light and stillness and regrets.

The logic of wicks made for a proper burn,
patches of light illuminating the gray,
the house seems lighter if no less solemn
now that the departed has returned home.
The diary contains cries of every color,
an orchard of thorn and briar and bane.
The academy of the future has closed doors.
It is unwilling—books banned, curtains drawn.

—after Jody Azzouni

shaped like crystalline balls
their ominous emptiness of color
sprout below eyelids, like
amber moons echoing fleshy desire
cultured in a medium of light
responding only to the fingers
angling for an itch

—after Marvin Bell

Freedom of all sorts.
Life, literally—if small.
Each time we thought we'd won/done
every humanly possible thing
grandly articulating our cause
in an arena of bones,
to rid ourselves forever
of the dreariest of realities,
the old bigotries re-enslaved us
and the old wars taunted "Fight!"
And some had already given till exhausted
for the sake of their children
and the future they'd never enjoy.
A designated few gained fame and
riches in the way of great martyrs
or potentates. Others died under jails
or within them, spiritless, spirited away
in the service of crime. Others
entombed themselves in bureaucratic or
corporate catacombs—any institution
open to shielding frightened deluded souls,
content to mutter platitudes on being
colorblind and safe, mollified with standing
still which bests not standing at all.

—after Michael Benedikt

1

Was the—

No.

Did they?

No.

Have you?

No.

What was—

It was.

Will you?

No.

Have you ever?

I don't recall.

Do you?

Yeah.

2.

May I?

No.

May I please?

No.

Aren't you?

Yes.

O are you?

Yes.

Do you?

Occasionally.

In that case, may I?

Uh-huh.

3.

Wuzzit?

Yes.

For sure?

Maybe.

Absolutely?

Perhaps.

I'm only 51% sure.

Are you in that deep?

Horribly.

Guilty or innocent?

Depends.

4.

Would you?

No.

I would.

Whatever makes your socks go up and down.

Do you care?

Don't have the time.

Does it matter?

I suppose.

But wouldn't you just love to?

Not at that speed, dear.

—after John Berryman

Here. He contemplates a solitude
neither desired nor romantic, an uncourted dark
in which he finds himself becalmed,
his pen not the poison kind,
and a gun too messy and commonplace.
He's not at all afraid, except that some idiot

might intrude and spoil that final discourse
between himself and his subtle bedeviler
as they merge in that mirror of a lake
all Christmas perfect in The Now
or shimmery in deep season's change.
Then. This is the dark he lives in,

grading grimly clumsy theses, coveting
co-eds in their blush, cursing the artless
rituals by which he's damned.
Wishing is a kind of dying and he has spent
his future crying in the drink
of his decline—an unnatural man.

CONSCIOUSNESS RAISING EXERCISE

—after Elizabeth Bishop

Think of the tornado roaming the nation uneasily
like tall blond boys in black coats with semi-
automatics taking names in a high school library.

Think how they must look now, the rotted innocents,
thinking they were safe, slain before they had the chances
most take for comfort if not for granted,

whose families will forever mourn by the light
of their faiths or the fires of their estrangements.
Think of the paths walked to the crossroads,

the solemn pledges, the good done, the vows, the smiles
revealed in photograph albums and mementos—small
things kept to stay the flood.

It's raining dirty water all over America. The hearths
of thousands are broken with countless fireplaces
cracked and gone to weed. The Arks are slowly filling

with unknown species and new breeds. What happened to
the brave? Have they departed with the free? Think of the
gutters crammed with souls gone needlessly to waste.

Think of hundreds seeping into history's tar
as still as redwood or mounds of shoes; think
of them, deeply injured, as disturbances unresolved.

—after Robert Bly

Countless dramas and bad weather from Nome
to Tampa Bay—the airwaves are polluted with a plague
of panderers & academic experts peddling books.

See the space shuttle spewing astronuggets,
the imported cars stealing jobs & dollars, the
Puritan Killer loosening his guns on grade school children.

Wild dogs tear off profits & women's breasts, run off
with the paycheck to the Bahamas or Montreal. The
          neutered
teams with neutered players listlessly scramble for balls.

A detective sells his hero-client, the Negro
prosecutor becomes a star to White viewers who like
their darkies on their side of the color bar.

The agitated filaments of the mind slowly separate.
The syntax bursts in a huff of hurt and rage
like the heart of Oklahoma as it suddenly explodes.

—after Borges, for Tessa Christensen

The useless savior finds me nailed to a rusty junk-
    yard chassis, I have outlived the light.
Sightseers once came in proud waves: laughter rang
    on the hilltops and multi-hued chatter
    filled this basin with breathy desire.
Young days have a habit of quarrelsome gifts and
    confusions, of promises half meant, half
    kept, of finding joy in flawed self-revelations.
    Days are like that, as if you didn't know.
That blasphemy, that brightness, left dots before my
    eyes and burnt off my lashes; a few respected
    enemies to chat with, art for brains, and
    stoked on freedom's promise. The kind of
    bulltripe & betrayal I've had a bellyful of
    (wrote like a Nigger, got paid like a Mexican).

You know who I am in your bones and why you must hate me.

Words, thoughtless snipes, your cruelty; and you,
    as icy a beauty as your Norwegian north. We
    argued and I will never forget your words.
The sheltering night finds me stranded on a vacant lot
    in the city of my dishonor & abuse.
Your smile is turned away, the sounds that compose
    your name, a bizarre cacophony: these are
    the broken memories you have left me.
I turn them over in the gravel, I lose them, I find
    them; I feed them to stray cats who vomit up
    fur balls and bits of gyrfalcon.

My dark rich life…

I must stain you, somehow. I must make enchantments
    from those broken memories you've left me. I want
    your hidden envy, your bitter smile—that greedy
    haunted regret your ugly mirror hoards.

2

What can I seduce you with?
I offer you alleyways, bitter sunrises, the
    unapologetic blaze of urban hope.
I offer you the sweet darkness of a woman who has
    looked too long into her lonely tarot
I offer you my slave ancestors, my beloved dead,
    the beauty living men have dishonored in head-
    lines: my father's terror of being lynched
    from the church steeples of Little Rock,
    Arkansas, my maternal great grandmother's
    callused feet after her walk along the Trail
    of Tears from Tennessee to Oklahoma territory,
    my maternal grandfather's miserly diggings
    in the dead of history to hide his fortune
    from his children, my cousin—just twenty-five—
    found dead in the workplace, her heart having
    stopped to leave her leaning over an indifferent
    corporate accounts ledger.
I offer you whatever incites my blood, whatever
    incurs my wrath or stirs my vision.
I offer you the spurned loyalty of a woman who
    has ever been the stupid loyal fool.
I offer you that kernel of myself—that unwanted
    playmate—that central core that deals not in
    dreams, but traffics in pain and is undiminished
    with time, knows no enjoyment—a wellspring
    of adversities.
I offer you the memory of stolen virginity, a rose
    violated under a mother's vigilant fear.

I offer you spells to relieve emptiness, incantations
    to calm troubles, surprising magics to delight
    the tongue and eye.
I give you my graciousness, my roundness, the feast
    of my words; I am trying to bribe you with
    certainty, with deliciousness, with victory.

—after David Bromige

He has painted her blue. They sit over brunch
in the calm of a winter's sun. "Quantum spirituality,"
someone coughs. "There's that story in this
Sunday's review," someone suggests, though neither

thought is conclusive nor limited to discourse
on the creation of unjust lives. Consider the woman
pushed into a premature splat by the sheep she's
herding. "That's corollary to unrecognized artistic

accomplishment," someone says. The champagne toast
is to this near-trampled victim of misguided enthusiasm
for work & impeded vision. "Worse ways to die,"
someone says. Like that woman innocently devoured by

the internal workings of a New York department store
escalator right before her children—the basest
price for the goose-step of Progress anyone might
unexpectedly pay at an inopportune moment. Like that

heedless schnook who, in the process of burglarizing
a haberdashery, unintentionally hung himself
by the yarn of his own sweater, snagged on a nail
and unraveled. But naught more cynically delicious

(ridiculous) than their existential plight/futile
reexaminations of their dilemma: Last night's
presumed immortality in morning's chilly light.
Someone asks, rhetorically of course,

"Geometry or God?"

178

BLOOD AROUSAL

—after O. Michael Brown

horizons no further than his side of our bed & mine
separate us in this black sky. these are the final hours

of my monthly bleedings. i feel his wanting to stem
the flow, to override the rush of my blood in his own

my ruined scarlet pouring out, absorbed & discarded
o rued hate-filled youth, don't let the door catch

yo bottom on da way out. what they do not tell
about marriage is how flesh-hunger deepens & sweetens

desire driven by the rhythms of repeated matings forms
habit, a dual intoxication, belly-to-belly joined in

sensual smashings dictated by rotations of bones—hips
knees elbows—hands grabbing fistfuls of hair & meat

what cannot be discussed is that eternal momentum
that ends in traveling spirals/oneness shared

where wordlessly twinned we hang on

—after Lewis Carroll

one midnight flight to Xanadu
   i got lost in the sky
the cloud i rode had quite a load
   that dwindled bye-and-bye
it made me late, a fact i hate
   but i've not learned to lie

by the time i got to Xanadu
   my night had turned to day
all the gold had turned to gilt
   and all the crystal, clay
the partyers were snoring bores
   the goodies stashed away

by the time i arrived in Xanadu
   sweet mama proved a crone
cracks and crannies sported dust
   and brambles maned the stone
and everything i thot was steel
   had crumbled as if bone

as i made my descent on Xanadu
   my bowels were in my throat
my hair was gray my hands were red
   and i couldn't sing a note
and as i warbled at the swans
   my last glass slipper broke

by the time i stormed drear Xanadu
   all the stories had been told
the mirth was spent, i hadn't a cent
   my courage was going cold

and when i touched the hand of God
   it simpered into mold

by the time i found lost Xanadu
   my rose had lost his bloom
the music men had packed and fled
   the dance floor was a tomb
and all the thrills that might've been
   were shrieking in the gloom

one midnight flight to Xanadu
   my heart fell from the sky
the cloud i rode had quite a load
   that dwindled bye-and-bye
which made me blue, but ever true
   for i've not learned to lie

—*after Sandra Cisneros*

before i rolled above the horizon, i was Pacifica.
i was the ghost of a shadow crossing a field
of disembodied eyes. i was the best years of a derelict
snotting into his callused palm. i was a drama without
catharsis. my essence ripened and flowered like
        a blue orchid in deepening shade

when i was a cloud, i listened to the birds, and the
things the birds sang. i was the soft fragrant blow
of baked bread in early morning, the spidery tickle
of a last autumn breeze. i was the inky industrial rain
peppering windshields in urban gridlock, that devilish jinn
that spun leaves furiously, stinging the legs and
cheeks of squealing children at play. i was sand,
skittering on a Mojave eddy. i was the color of love

and when

i opened my heart to the earth, across the cracked cement
of an embittered youth, those double rainbows lit my being

and i joined cold ether

—after Tom Clark

the honeypot becomes so sweet under his tongue
it strengthens his arousal and at the same
time causes him to lick harder, which stimulates
her further richness to facilitate a mounting
moistness. her orgasm fairly pulls him under as he
thrills to the duet of sphincter & cervix—
the inexpressible pleasure of her contractions
inspired by him—as she melds beyond complete relaxation
in too exquisite a surrender, her body opened and
well-lubricated, welcoming the easy thrust of his hips
in a spell of satisfaction, knowing yet another wave
of pleasure awaits her as his penis glides/rides
the residuals of her first wave, daring her. more

—after Francine Coneley

i'm so big i can barely walk. i wear
tent dresses for coolness and comfort.
i rock 'n' roll, stumble 'n' scoot. when
some man likes me, he says "Hotcha Big Mama!"
when he teases, he says the same

i live everywhere at once. hot pink mules
toast my feet. my hair is braided tight
against my scalp under this'n wig.
'girlfriend this and girlfriend that,
skinny men prefer 'em fat.' my good good
cookin' keeps folk comin' round. when
i stomp my foot the ducks take ground

i relax by sitting for so long
staring at the TV screen, reading my
fanzine, making sweet things for dessert,
'tween frettin's why can't i make this life work

when i walk too much too slow, i sweat head-to-toe
my heart thumps in my neck, my arches
threaten to fall. i gasp

the only safe stairway for me to climb
is in my dreams. sometimes the world fits
and though i can't be called small
no one laughs or cracks jokes behind my back

    i will cut you
    with my tongue
    my nails and the
    butcher's knife
    in that order

when i sit on concrete, it gives
when i sit on a man, he disappears

i have pretty eyes, they say

when i stomp my foot, the ducks take ground

–after Gregory Corso

spinning tall tales as sizable luminaries
bide their time:

Her mom cooked her dad. There was so much blue smoke,
no one could think.
Drinking buddies had the whew-awful job
of removing the crust and cooling him off.

toxic vibes

Being Black Myself

harbinger of light, my third-eye shine

refreshing, as he
sinks vagina deep into
pulsating confusions fostered by truths dropped like bombs
reducing congas to table tops
the boom and bust of unreal estate

jockeying progressive transformations

calabash, pumpkin and a yam sort of glory
nostalgic for those boogie-woogie boys & big band
            impresarios

i am sweet river where the nightstroker drinks my water
(drinks me out of my mind)
him—a rock forged of flesh. he provides

my nightly dose of hope in flame's place

186

—after James Dickey

Here they are. Pages wide open.
If they have lived in a word
It is The Word.
If they have lived on lips
It is in rolling alliteration
Bringing listeners to their feet.

Having no substance, they have come,
Anyway, beyond all knowing
As if instinctual or organic
And they rise.
The pages wide open.

To speak them, to embrace them,
Thinking desperately
Formulating theories, stories & laws
That—then doing is required:
The richest thought
The most profound.

For some of these,
This will never be the place
Our hate-filled streets stink
With the blood of innocents
And ideas are banned or burned
When they are feared.

More deadly than one might think
They must be considered quietly
In privacy, alone or in cabals
Should they be called dissent or indecent
And such thinkers demonized.

For certain ideas to find the light
It may take a millennium
And those haunted by them
Know this is their life.
Their reward: to walk

Under the shadow of Knowledge
Deprived of all greatness
And to feel, not joy
But resentment and disgust
Engorged with mental pain.

Yet they return. The wise eyes open.
If repressed they tremble
Under the need
They rise, torn from history
They rise and don flesh again.

—after George Evans

on a dark plain (call it smoke) in a
    city of closets
    he makes faces
in the mirror, carries a switchblade
    in his boot, owns
    a bomber's jacket
vintage Viet Nam, last served time for
    possession
    two years ago.
sometime in county jail among a cage
    full of Black
    and Mexican youths
taunting each other between longings
    for escape and
    peanut butter &
jelly sandwiches most of whom have never
    seen the insides
    of a real restaurant
or smelled a perfumed thigh—really bad
    daddies & vatos.
    the Blacks knew he
was Black but the Mexicans thought
    he was an S.A.
    with all that wavy
hair & shit (he never complained they
    could take him for
    whatever they took
him for. he was cool either way). the white
    bread gummy
    with rancid
brown sludge on the verge of separation
    and a layer

of strawberry
jam as thin as the glue on the backside
          of a postage stamp
          and warm orange
juice or worse, warm milk as in "fresh
          from Mama's titty"
          though what he
hungered for most was pizza and a cold
          Beck's dark
          after sucking
the peace out of a fat j. women are drawn
          to the need
          he puts in his eyes
like a bull calf. he always works with
          a partner when
          moonlighting.
someone's got to cover his back. when he
          sleeps he dreams
          about ocean surf
that he's riding in on the last wave
          gripped by the
          pleasure of his
glide, he hangs there above the universe
          then takes the
          promise of her
touch. water flows. and he turns over
          in the wetness.
          but she's changed
into a parole officer lecturing him on
          the remedies for
          worthlessness
and incorrigibility. release into the
          minions is the
          next best thing
to sex, no doubt, they'll be together soon.
          soon is now/

the principle of
attraction. "How much longing is inspired,
 in particular,
 by all the things
one is deprived of?" soon is repeated drives
 to Long Beach
 walks along the
shore, star struck under the southwestern
 moon. the last
 score was solid.
he's in pocket, can hear the admonishment
 of the parole
 officer for his
lack of respect for the property of others.
 he's liberated
 enough money and
dope to see him through a while and take
 the worry from
 her eyes, which
have become the taillights of a camper
 making its way
 north to Big Sur.
across the universe (call it Hollywood)
 he can hear the
 loud laughter
of working class men chatting over boiler-
 makers, chewing
 over the cup size
of the doozy who gets off at one-forty-five.
 no one ever
 thinks to bring
her flowers and she no longer cares. but
 when he smiles
 at her, it damn
near stops her heart. soon now. and he
 stares at, then

through the mug
(call it a crystal ball) and sees a man
        pushing a food
        cart down a cold
gray corridor, an absurdly old man
        with brick-hard
        muscles, balding
up top, with what's left of his hair in
        a ponytail down
        to his ass. Popeye
the cart pusher, moving as fast as he
        can, yet never
        gets there. soon
is now. the fifth menthol stick because
        it feels good at
        the back of his
throat and prolongs the high. the air is
        heavy with water
        rain coming
a storm blown in off the big island crashing
        stateside, big
        and nasty. he
could've been a character actor with
        looks like those,
        scary looks as
in he'd sooner fillet a man's rib cage
        than clean his
        nails with that
switchblade. who are we kidding? they
        beat the shit out
        of him when he
was a kid because he was too light to be
        one of them and
        too dark to pass

192

—after Lisa Fineberg

we sampled refuge under bent neon
behind heartbreak's walls
desire deep in the other's skin/the mattress
betrayed us as fresh versions of a time-worn lyric—
my spanking new r&b received his hard rock
going down the chart as Tom Petty set
the basecount, "you got lucky babe, when..."
we found the melodic line and broke it
across our flanks like rebellious electric guitars
against hungry amps, softness followed
silence in that restless wanting gap. he
begged me to lie but i told the truth

—after Allen Ginsberg

what bohunkian images i have of you
crash against my niggernoggin as i shiver and stroll
long air-conditioned aisles at 2 a.m. the liquor
under lock and key, the lettuce full and moist with
a fresh spray of mist and neon
my cart wobbles giddily on crooked wheels as i sputter
between the confused and the absurd as i cruise for
            pudding
and citrus-free hand lotion. there's plenty of disabled
parking outside. it is lonely here though the
automatic doors never close and a bleak phosphorescence
never dims and bananas are going at two pounds for
the price of one. the bin of avocados is small
and most of them more like plankton-stained golf balls
or too rotten. somewhere, i am detected via camera
lens while picking over pepper mills between
the spice racks and the baking soda

hang ten toward checkout is a certainty

the only Walt here is Disney
the pork chops are killing me
i am a nobody angel
my heart is a frozen delicacy

—after Louise Gluck

Fish nets walked the waves of Santa Monica.
And there were neon signs
by which The Cheetah wooed us, by starlight, wooed us
by Night: among the martinis—
an uncurable cottonmouth that caused the tongue
to roll up tight and the throat
to close. Rebirth, not death, is the hard lot.
I know. I got away, just barely, with my spots.

—after Paul Goodman

"Cabby, what dream is this?" I asked, well knowing
it was our ceaseless nightmare showing
"It is our effing horror flick," he said, then crowing
"And I know all the outs and ins."

My heart I fairly spat, and on my tongue it sat
suffrage to select this glory,
"I'd appreciate another spin before day starts growing,"
and I waved a wad of bills beneath his chin.

"Rider, this is the route we take to get our muffins
baked, if breakfast's the story."
"No, no!" I fairly sputtered, "Night is what I fancy!
Loud music, thick smoke and cheap perfume!"

Thus we're driving still, threadbare tires showing
under the purple-black cloud-dotted sky
singing classic rock, swigging wine and toking.
Sleep tight, dear one. We've landed on Andromeda.

—after Donald Hall

If 'twas said, "Little knives
work as well as double
edged-blades, depending
on the task. A soft
yielding throat may give

with almost no pressure
whereas mid-torso
can dull the staunchest
saw," they'd smile,
assured matters culinary

were at hand, and
forget the wild slow
chase in the streets, the
calls containing threats of
self-murder and eternal

grief. Because we remain
uprooted and denied control, trapped by
any symbol thrust into the media
like a knife or fallen hero or
the ass-kissing jokers

whose words stab and
butcher our truth
to entertain the crowds who,
before buying tickets,
peek in from the white sidewalks.

—after Anthony Hecht

Catching a twist on a savage shimmy down
'Twas a time of pot-smoking & house parties—
Double o Soul. The blind passion of bones
        knocking grandly,

A rousing time had by Shorty Long & Lone.
Bad raps & signifying were ways of life.
That was the time I came into my own.
        Black Power we cried.

Feet were feverish with dance & rebellion,
Hands to hips or hurling bricks, youth
Bursting free of the bondage that had held a
        generation's tongue.

Only a day to live but live it the max.
Experiment and open wide and drink it strong.
To the victor goes the loot & all the guns
        and sex to boot.

Boldness synonymous with black leather & tams.
Waves & ringlets crowning a nation of Nefertitis
With exuberant visions on the rise, dusky
        pearls & black thighs.

Some were smote by the mighty light of fame,
others fell from grace and left a trail of shame.
A few left for foreign lands, leaving The Lames
        to deal with The Man.

'Twas the last cool wave 'fore daybreak hit

And scattered those contagious dreams,
That began the reign of serious heat which burned
all blossoms in the steam.

—after Anthony Hecht

During the Plague of Lies I lost one of my own.
It was a time of mounting tensions in my home—
We had no protection. The laughing skull of bone
            grinned its welcome

Like a good Republican with special interest in my kind.
Dunners called daily, creditors were denied.
That was the period in which I lost my stateliness of mind.
            All my income died.

The symptoms—a deepening darkness round the eyes,
A constant need to talk, a short rope at the neck
Sleepless around the clock, not knowing wrong from wise—
            in turn, completely wrecked.

One could live years with the virus before you're dead.
But the most curious prelude is that solitary dance
Most victims do, cut off from life, out of sight/unread
            without a decent glance

To make what's left of their time worth the paraphasic
            gasp—
Of having taken a breath at all. They're ignored till dry,
If not old, in an academically bureaucratic grasp
            and cannot fathom why.

Some, caught in these convolutions, have been known
To leap from windows, to fly. Others are forever
Awash in whirlpools, dancing on the hellish foam
            no longer seen as clever

If seen at all. But for what punishment, there go I?
Powerless against the vapors, madly thrashing in a fit
Bemoaning the unfinished works & unpenned lives
yet damned for having written.

—after Jane Hirschfield

she is dreaming now, in her lust-ridden room
unlike this one,
the one where she writes what no one reads.

her life is strewn with yellowing paper.
the maroon of night would be welcomed
but only stagnant gray streams thru slanted blinds,
reveals a sulky discourse, burnt umber eyes
plowing memory for threads of joy,
anguish scalp-deep, yet unswimmable.

and when she caws for rescue, only the white crow
caws back outside her secret window

(she imagines this is Madrid
the poets have gathered in the square
she is among them, silent & smiling
the evening closes round. "ah, *this* is
a lovely eternity," she thinks)

her chair is as black as thunderheads
roiling above Mount Wilson, a promised storm.
the coiled neck of the lamp snakes
as if looping its lost Eden, tempting her
to partake of forbidden drama. too near
her office door lingers the scent of
her just-absented lover, the hint of a mystery
to which her yearnings are joined

her mistakes appear, luminescent children
sudden tuggings at her toast-brown fingertips
needy eyes aglow with a distant criminal hurt

(her room is bathed in music because her love requires
        music)

o my heart sunk in its gorge deluge

her desk is vortex in which the aleph appears
the leaving of stressful sleeplessness
or the residual chill of a waning dawn.

a lyric settles in by the shade of a pica
a rage of diphthongs savage the page

yet
on grief's flood, her bridge to the past
is rained away
in torrential screams. and there's not
paper enough, in this reality, either to reconstruct it
or stem the skyburst

—after Jack Hirschman

it was an unusual morning
his birth into blackness
thirty-two years ago, my
blond-skinned freckled son

how thinly bronze his hair
when i clipped it
for saving. how cold
his whitened cheek to my lips

i sit in the bleeding light
shredded by memories
he's nearly one year gone
a shrieking blink

yet every day i hear
his reedy voice on ether & wind
the gilded laughter
of his pleading love.

five years old. proud
man of the house. the key
around his neck. left to
protect his sister in
an unforgiven past

—after Randall Jarrell

One looks and looks from behind the door
the dark child frightened by daylight.
What is unseen still massacres.
Nothing is safe. There are devil winds and
giant eyeballs and walking corpses dripping
gray in the dull ending of a summer's day.

Outside the door, the warped
distortion of mundane things
deceives the blinking watcher.
Utility poles spook the blue,
evergreens offer sinister shade—
a suspect neighborhood—*that*
to the childish one is plain.
Beyond the door, the passing
strangers glide through, swiftly
toward a foreign realm to joust
the tyranny of time, the dangers
to their lives ill-perceived, the
mangler's hands alabaster

and thick, there's quick murder
awaiting them in unmade beds.
Beyond the door, intruders prowl
and thieves who'll snatch one's
tonsils out. Ogres and swamp goblins
wiggle and slurp, a true bestiary
of brutes. Cookies and gingerbread
signal certain doom. The spider woman
draped in stars will suffocate
unwary travelers in her wicked web.
Beware! They're going to get you

in the twinkle of a rhyme. This
child-fear, not unlike the knot of woe
that ruins the tummy and the rug.
It's out there. Behind everything.
Malevolent, nefarious, corrupt.

—after Denise Levertov

The unread poems of true poets
are sad. No one should love
so hard in vain and go unnoticed.
This sunset should trouble
the sky. Rip the curtains
from the windows and shout
It's their fault!—the craven curs
around and around and all fall
down everywhere, the gut-rending
sound of cogs grinding and poets
felled silent. If the empty only
feed the empty, the reign
of apathy will go on and Molochs
triumph. True poets will go on,
unread, eking out a space at the mean
end of time. They will bare their
teeth and spring at the moon.

–after Jane Miller, for Jokie X Wilson

of the pains this indifferent Union
       offers
i never thought i'd bear the weight
of a dying son—or the debt

when i was pregnant
birthing my child seemed a lovely loving
       start to
life anew, not knowing love would not offset
       poverty
not knowing art and desire would not
       feed us
and dreams weren't enough to give
us all we'd soon desperately require

thirty-two years of struggle—the great price

late this afternoon, three years after
the scattering of ashes,
i found a poet's song among the sheets
of long-canceled accounts, the nude torsos
of muscular men and several clippings.

one reports the increased number
       of weddings
of men to men, one male bride smiling at his groom
over glasses of champagne
we believe in god the caption shouts.
       in yet another,
a dead dog returns to its owner, dripping
acid rain on the carpet.
       another

describes the Pentagon's failure to test a possible cure
an infected actor undergoes religious conversion
a homosexual spy sues the FBI
a sailorboy is murdered under the fists
         of five of his mates

among them i find
my son's paean to the god of fire
an ad for Eternity
the hospice admissions agreement
a photograph of a photograph of Marlene Dietrich
is our sexual and behavioral fate in our genes?
         another caption asks

                   what has made
         and kept us the freak children of the universe?

what evil says our deaths are deserved?

the California shore is along the ring of fire
where new earth forms
shaking loose the old, reminder to
         the living—
nothing is solid or unshakable
to know blackness is to know bereavement
         hence
the price/taxation for each blessed breath

as we tear at our hearts and our skins
as we grope among one another
among denials cruelties horrors
         awestruck
and stumbling against the invisible

—after Howard Moss

They've been telling me who I am
all my life: black, ugly & unwanted—
more alien than aliens and yet, native.
From afar, I've heard the familiar
harangue, have shaped it into songs
and sonnets, turned its confusion upside
into art. Yet still it comes from
everywhere without decrease in volume.
The thunder of hatred beats me dim,
its rank discordance ruins the things
I love, turns all romances grim.

The barriers I build against it resound
and crumble, and screaming for their
lives, my comrades run. From me. Afraid
they, too, will be unfairly stained by my
fate. Black and ugly and more alien than
native born, subject to ceaseless harangue.

> *"I have taken such a large dose of crap*
> *and still feel nothing. a slight light-*
> *headedness, but no damage, unless*
> *numbness of the toes is a warning sign.*
> *Strange. And several centuries have*
> *passed. The terrible world rages on.*
> *And I am doubled up with constant cramps,*
> *and yet ultimate death seems far away..."*

210

—after Stanley Moss

Building a lexicon of my precious dead
something like embracing an ocean
my heart takes in the water.
There's no relief, but I refuse the flood
and sling my bucket possessed and mad and wet and
drowning, racked with sleeplessness
continuing to force love through glumness
my creation a fury married to the wind
in dark ritual of blood rain
I ride my broom, I whip my broom
dragon wings rip at my shoulders
I have not used my blackness well.

TO THE HEAD NIGGER WENCH IN CHARGE

—after Frank O'Hara

I wanted to be sure I left my mark on you;
though time was precious and the margin
for the success of my escape becoming
narrower by the second. It wasn't my intent
to kill you, although that would've been easy
enough, or to maim. So when you froze in
the flash of my blade, you needn't have wet
your pants. Altho throwing up your arm in
self-defense was opportune. It allowed
me to slice you once quite cleanly, and then be
on my way, the hounds in my wake, the bounty
hunters salivating over the price my hide will
bring. And I may be shot or I may swing.
But you'll wear my mark until your dying hour—
a reminder that you're a traitor to humankind.
And you'll hear my laughter rising from the hell
between your ears and curse my black behind.

—after Kenneth Patchen

This year grave grass covers the innocent.
We stand now, and grieve;
the future stolen before our eyes; betting on
the state-run numbers racket; drinking sugarless java.
We have too much to do; nowhere and nobody's help.

Last year echoed the year before; a debt unpaid.
They called us 'old souls,' street-wise & cool.

We manage to maintain that look young women have;
Earthy hunger smolders behind our eyes and breasts.

We will probably shout & hallelujah when we die.
We were never accepted all the way—as whole women.

We are the insulted, sister, the desolate dames.
Dreamwalkers in a dark and terrible waking,
where the multitudes define us with dirty lies.
Cold points measure us, Lady
The cold points of the law

—after Kenneth Patchen, for Sylvia

It is big.
How does a shattered family
hear the whisper of death?
Cope with
its troubling woo?

It is big. Inside a small room
soft & terrible in its warmth.
In him.
Shadows under the skin,
the history of a process.

It is big.
In this scenario, a son.
Like the giddiness of paddling
a skiff along a tributary of the Amazon.
Like being there to cheer
when Check Point Charlie is closed.
As big as
cramming all one dreams into
a single wink of sleep. As big as
morphine stemming mortal pain.
In him. Shadows.

It is big
inside a mother. It is soft and beautiful
on her child's face.

In him.

EXILED TO THE OUTSKIRTS

—after Leroy Quintana

tough luck is being born in post-war Los Angeles
and turning thirteen in the middle
of the civil rights movement
life complicated by the hazards of kinky hair
and the hardships of big bones, fat genes and an insatiable
lust for the boys

tough luck. you smell like fried hair pomade, calamine lotion
and Vicks VapoRub

no one's willing to touch you except mom and dad

tough luck. no one comes here, promptly at seven a.m.
to save you from indoctrination
on Sunday mornings.
tough luck. no one tells you that it's too-cool
to love books. to love poetry. to love yourself.
tough luck. no one tells you that you have a hellish beauty
uniquely darkly yours

there's no one able to teach you about making money

tough luck. you are left alone to unscramble all eggs
for yourself. tough luck. there is no one to save you from
the conga rhythms inside your head.
tough luck. everything about you seems an anathema.
and those hands—people tell you they
look like they belong on a monkey

(remember that time at the funeral. when you
touched Great-grand Aunt Cora's hand, she snatched hers
away and left yours stroking the air)

there's no one. no one at all who will sit next to you
on the city bus or the church pew

you go home alone to be at home alone

inside your head

you have the White world's permission to commit suicide
                anytime
you feel like it. the sooner the better

plunge in at any point. drown in the heavy-heartedness

—after Sylvia Rosen

outside the wind buffets the ghost of a patio
the pine blooms, renewed by the winter's heavy
rainfall, new moss and grasses are startled up from mud
and a slender ficus sapling recalls the tenuous bond
between the dead father and the living daughter.
listen. squirrels and pigeons are nuzzled in and stilled
opulent-furred cats lounge on the studio futon

this is a dream i can't recall

except that this is a Wednesday
and another month
slips into the unnerving past

soft shivers come on the "hooo" of the unseen owl

urbane & weary, i should be enchanted
i'm haunted instead, afraid
of the unlit candle which bursts spontaneously
into flame, afraid of the voice that speaks from the
photograph, afraid of the whisper
at the bottom of my cup. silence has
transformed itself into absence, memory
into mystery, loss into more loss

soft shivers come on the "hooo," an owl unseen

behind the sliding door a twisting & turning
proceeds. hands dance uselessly to the familiar
rhythms & blues of a bygone willfulness
never happy, never self-deceived but calm and sure.
there's the rustling of a flutter in a dresser drawer

217

the resonant hum of unused crystal stemware
as the desire for escape descends on the dust

as i recall, tenuously, the bond between
the dead son and the living mother

another door closed against the wind

impenetrable by flesh

—after Anne Sexton

I went out to possess the spirit of women
when it was bitch & butch, feeling the
bold itch to write. Sexton and Plath were
long dead, but there she was—her renown
was named Ann. And it didn't matter
if I was of a different race, she
handled my fire with a learned grace.

She was a mere snip of a lady in her
size two dress and mushrooms, with
graying flaxen hair. And the room
was crammed with nymphal poets
like myself, and we leaned into our
elbows, hushed our competition for
her eyes, and scribbled sacred notes.

Two-thirds into the lecture one lass
finally asked, "Where do you get ideas
for poems?" Ann pantomimed the act. "I open
Webster's Dictionary," she entoned, "and at
random, let my finger fall upon a word. And
I think upon that word until upon my page
a poem has bled." With that, I promptly
dropped my pen and in a snit I fled.

—after Karl Shapiro

My soul stands at the window of my success
And I ten thousand deaths away;
My days are filled with sleep-stealing stress
Salt soaks for feet, a bitter remedy.
Let the planet crack for the wasted dead.

My unselfish youth, my books with tattered edge,
Knowledge is my gaze down ghetto streets.
Boys who dared the White world's ledge,
Girls pregnant with a sullen hope, yet sweet.
Let the planet crack for the wasted dead.

My night remains night, my night his day.
So we lie down, part my thighs.
The love burns deep, the stars give way.
The come brings down the firmament.
Let the planet crack, for the wasted die.

Grief is now my way of foot of hand of heart.
A gallows laughter marks my stride;
My face grown hard like ebony quartz,
My bloodshot eyes at dawn must ride.
Let the planet crack for the wasted dead.

AROUSED

—*after Charles Simic*

Elephant heart throbs—a drum's thunder.
It rains loads of toads.
Thru dark inner cities afire, I lead
the flames, climb the sky, roar.
Tall things crumble to ashes and almost
nothing will remain but the dishonest talk of fools.

When the sun & smiles return, happy shoppers
will pick over the past at market's open.

The shadows of hyenas occlude my vision.
My legs are tightly concealed under my skirt,
my hands in a fury of strokes to banish falsity.
Bones knock and shiver roughly
against each other hungrily.

All that hung limp is hard with life.

—after William Stafford

Traveling through the dark, I found a lover
determined to tame my melane wilderness.
It is usually best to approach me cautiously
but he zeroed in like planetshakers.

Under a glow, we stumbled to my squeekmobile
and washed the windshield in our steam.
He had stiffened, hot to groove. I drove us
back to his haunt to give Romeo a thrill.

His fingers touched me in places untouched
and stripped me of my reservations. I lay there
breathless as if expired, yet more alive
than I had been since who remembers when?

And lo! He liked sex with the lights ablaze
he wanted to see, not imagine. A libidinal
pragmatist! I did not hesitate and reclined
naked in a glaze of satyr's eyes & lightbulbs.

I thought hard about us, as he had made me
his, and shot my better sense into orbit.

—after Mark Strand

In this country
I am the absence
of country.
This is
the unfortunate case.
Wherever I am
I am what is seen but ignored.

When I walk
I part the eyes
and always
the heads whirl
to fill the gap
where my history's inscribed.

I have hoarded all the reasons
for a crackling
wall of flame.
I move
to keep thangs up front.

—after Sun Ra, for Gloria Macklin

In the early days of my earthly visitation,
Black hands slapped me and spanked me...
Black minds, hearts and souls rebuffed me...
yet I loved them hungrily, in spite of that.

In the early days of my visitation
Black lips called me names, as did White lips
but somehow, those names on those Black lips
impaled me like spears on which I forever writhe.

I became a name caller.

The hearts, minds and souls of my kin were denied me—
even today the overtones from the fire
of that lovelessness still burn in my brain.
I am twisted and hurt and death-damaged.

Yes—in those early days of my visitation
White rules and laws segregated me also,
but Black fear, ignorance and self-loathing
separated my soundness from my spiritfist.

And so
the strength I pray for and the freedom I seek
bear convolutions heretofore unaddressed, make
me the radical's radical, inspire a sacrifice so deep
it rattles the old bones and the old stones.

I am the Reaper's scythe. Unforgiving in my sweep.
I am. Because of that. Not long ago enough. Twisted
and hurt and damaged.

—after James Tate

Your face never wore a frown
like those others—the dark men
who in their goings nowhere

today, riled and shook their
fists against tomorrow. Your
face was implacable and smooth

like the slab under which you lie,
an ebony granite that throws
back the sky and clouds overhead

and draws the water from my eyes.
But you refused to contemplate
your life's extinction, for rebirth

awaited you, the good son, loyal
(if not faithful) lover and father
of four. "Pure of heart" applied to

you, and the more cunning of your
friends considered you the fool
a man whose faith was not only in

God, but extended to mankind. And
they deserted after they'd had their
use of you. And I am in your image.

Pondering the loneliness that like-
wise shaped your fate. (And your
mother's.) What vision is this?

225

My dowry of unheralded calls.
Only to hear you whisper some banal
reassurance: "Vengeance is mine,

Sayeth..." And I accept your gift
of platitudes in a fierce defiant
silence as my stomach bites my soles.

The ground is damp and its loamy
warmth reminds me of the strength
and comfort of your grip. How is it

such beauty was never captured on film
or shown the world? Travesty is travesty
and all the comic laughter in nigger

heaven cannot mute the horror of lives
wasted in the service of race hate & greed.
Dad—there was nothing I could steal to

save you, as there is nothing I can
steal to save myself. You taught us
your cornbread & black-eyed pea Southern

way of being too well. Like you, it's
gotten us cursed & kicked by the SOBs,
devalued and blued, reduced, discarded.

And so, sunset finds me skirt hiked up,
legs irritated by the grass, cleaning
granite with spit and a rag. All I have.

—after Constance Urdang

What have I wrought
monsters
who roar like dragons bellowing
tall like the legendary giants of medieval
eastern Europe
death-dealers
who chase the villagers and tear up the
townships—
monsters sprouting everywhen (flying batlike on
impossible wings) petulant
gargoyle-tots
              volcanic—
dark sulphuric
brood
blood angels flying
monsters roiling in a new Pacific
where it bubbles with a strange
rare light
and slow sleepy monsters
heavy-lidded
nod in seclusion
hot cold wet dry hard harder
sharks who see through all/
naked revelations
eyeless embraces
authentic
unapologetic

Oh, bite, teeth!
Flap, wings!
Claw, Scratch! (Wham!

Hiss! Awk! Slap!!) thuD
                    R
                      E
                        A
                          M
                            E
                              R

made
poems made
monstrous

—after Peter Viereck

My eight PhDs invited me into their tower
Each had ruled a tenured seat in untold zones
Years of compromise, years of cowardice,
Of Hades' tenured self-exile on cushy privileged thrones.
My seven PhDs had forgotten what language is;
My eighth was a *willsee* (if he behaves his sunburnt bones,

We will see if he's fully accepted in our delusion).
The department had a banner up. Its welcome read "POET
    ACCEPTS CHARITY."
The chairperson made her speech, and virgin minds
    rainbowed classrooms
In the whorish multicultural spectacle of racial diversity.
But, though seven colleagues (plus Mr. Willsee) enviously
    EYED my parity,
They only filed venomous fangs; the seventh, a deposed
    chair foamed,

Fumed and frothed. How dare a self-made writer outpublish
    our
Entire kingdom of educated fools, no matter what her style
Or motivations. Damn her! Doesn't she know she's doomed
    to the impotence
That makes jokes of Sabbaticals & Summers, and turns us
    into crocodiles?
My eight China cups were waiting, with black tea of the soul;
And all was ready as my PhDs tramped in. They did not
    smile.

"Yo! Husks of former Novelists & Poets from Bygone
Youth," I said, "Relax and romp and know you're respected.
It's been a tough road to hoe since the deaths of JFK,

RFK and MLK—but Sophia's seasoned the gumbo—its
     protected
With her palms and her heart, so don't be gruesome; let's
Put on the jazz, cut the cake and get The Gone elected."

Did they cop jive? No way, Jose. They only passed the ballot
And labeled me a washout. Then they turned their asses
     high. Two
Swung from Shakespeare and pounced on the neotraditional.
Two held out for deconstructionist dada-doo-doo on the sly.
Pound became an issue as did Melville and Bishop, but I
Couldn't stain the core curriculum no matter how hard I
     dyed.

"I can get it for you wholesale doin' the dozens.
You can eat peanut P-Nut buttah, even sip the honeyed wine.
But whoever chips—no matter who—my China, dollface,
Will get riddled for the griddle in a fit
     of monkeyshine."
"No matter who?" the seventh asked—and tripped me
Right across the tea leaves. He broke my bountiful behind.

I awoke on this hellish, one-palmed stucco atoll
In a perfect climate full of bananas, beer & Thai food,
Where my sense of humor's tested by the silence
And I've nothing else to do but write and brood.
"Assholes, don't show your faces or I'll spit fire!"
Of course they couldn't read me. No one understood.

—after David Wagoner

A noose at your neck and a cross above your head,
You have gone to your maker with bared feet swinging
In air, wearing your blackness for and against desire, your
    beauty
And prowess hanging cruelly there, gaping, amazing the
Youthful passerby who sees in you his double, a like Fate,
And, oh, on that day, must wish himself safe in his own skin.

The weepers christened you Little Rock Boy. You were
    eighteen,
Eighty-five years ago, when you were lynched in a glacial
    rage,
Strangled as if a pupa trapped in a flawed chrysalis,
    enshelled,
An aborted Messiah, one less parter-of-seas long carrion
A bag of bones for the pluck-and-feed of condors. You
    believed in your Lord,
And met him by the white hands of base hate. You became
    what they feared.

He loved his bones and his own creaturely husk
But to save them meant abandoning the soil he loved.
Without safety, without decent shoes, in dirty coveralls
Snotting and bareheaded, undereducated but with bull's
    heart—
With sharp eyes, good ears, and a sweetly somber throat, he
    fled.
Taking everything. Nothing in his arms.

231

—after Diane Wakoski

She walks the purple carpet into my eyes
carrying the thirty pieces of silver
but an airplane rumbles overhead,
leaving its streamlined fantasy on my soul
and old aches   the endless rings of a telephone on hot
                                                afternoons
      no one answers, and that fact is a giant fly buzzing
thru my consciousness, stirring up murderous swats.

Loan me a hundred, she said,
from inside his boxes, those sorry imitations of Cornell
ashamed of her wig of Italian hair, explaining
that nappy heads have to work. Of course, I understand. But
they are about to cut off her lifeline. And her hands
pick at the hair every second, like whiskers on a cat,
inside her old head, too many acid trips, a ruined mouth
            where

                                                she
grinds her teeth when she chatters endlessly
about nothing on the phone, and writing anthems
that no one will ever hail. She's too mature to expect a music
                                          career.
I cannot let her walk inside me too long
the muscles in my stomach knot and
I heave.
I must reach down and pull her out
like a writhing asp
from my breasts.

—after Theodore Weiss

Late autumn's gold intensifies all things
so that rust is embronzed and I am found
within the battle scene, to see myself as if
painted by the flames of Georges de La Tour
and sitting with a tremulous tear glistening
at my eye, three glittering candles create
a crown of light around my head, held no doubt
by a foolish self-belief, my black unruly mass
of locks reddened, but held as well it seems,
by what I do, and by the urban blues I sing,
I moan it too,
                as one should wring
the moanin' out of a note—oh, let me sing it
beyond the reach of light, my glance, entwined
in my word's weaving, lit up, radiant in late
autumn's lusty close, my yearnings made visible
hovering in the gleam of spittle on my sassy
lips, spilling a telltale smile
from my shy sly skull, that all things
eagerly like lovers under the moon
attain their story, have it listened to,
spun glory from my lips and hands, my relentless
will, and still, as I am nestled
in behind my shield, like javelins thrust
thru the ether, I spin.

Ah, let this be a lasting vision:
this world's most blessed moment
from the sleight-of-hand of a poet,
and by her passion held in common, as if
all were children, naive and unspoiled,
excited by dreams to come, ballads

of first loves, the clouds and storms
of those first sweet betrayals, and
all the fires inside mere buddings of
our everlasting sigh;
                              think
nothing of the shroud, not yet the
frailties such opulence must breed; nor
think of loss, until now
wounded or spent among the weak of breath
without consent, a gleaming thread
in Fate's design, unraveling, my web—
torn and bloodied by the acts of war,
shield pierced, a heap of ruined rag—
and, last, the weaver of yarn from marrow

—after Reed Whittemore

It must be explained why it is in broad daylight,
    in our own home,
Even when no one's on the telephone, we feel
    we must whisper.
Masters & Johnson would've called it an act
    of repressed adolescent
Guilt. We think: others would call it perverse;
    it is probably
Something of both. In our bedroom, there are things we do
    we'd rather not discuss
In the bright of day.

We'd prefer to lie very still on the bed, watching
The television or reading reports on the culture—
The clock, the tissue box, the cigarettes—
Come alive.
Not as in some drug-induced hallucination,
    the dresser drawers
Opening and closing by themselves, or
Ali Baba riding his carpet thru the fragrant gloom,
But with religiosity, a routine of silence
Presided over by a seriously erotic entity or priest
Before a solemn joining of two greedy lovers
On the margins of a cruelty too obscene
    to grace with words
From his homage to Kandinsky mounting our wall
To the deep crimson piano and its stolid bench.

We find these rituals
Remarkable for their youthfulness and intensity,
    and we wish
    we might somehow

Preserve our physical eloquence, say, forever.
But always the couplings end, desire retracts, giving
tongues part.

A sigh, a smile shared.

—after Richard Wilbur

Bright bulbs & red neon LIQs sputter then wink out
And whole cities go soft, smoky and damp
Gliding flesh on flesh
To the swampy evocations of a dusky vamp,

And the soul rises. The soul rises and howls
A day's caustic news, alley fodder for rats—a crash
And the grind of timid hearts under steel-belteds,
Flattened to join the curbside trash.

Unruly youths fight the dark, deface statues
Of dead ideas, spit-defiant dogs
Who urinate against the world they'll
Never own, boots bracing stirrups on expensive hogs,

Ignoble arrogant dukes, carving their initials
Across the vision of a fourth estate
Listing down the pitted asphalt of capitals
Splitting ears and rattling all the pates.

Fuck you! Fuck you! Eff the megacorporate void!
But it's far too late, for the rabble wraps its wings
Around the torrid golden dollar sign
And masturbates until the avaricious eagle sings.

From roof to roof, false postulates
And the prayers of hypocrites create a din
That saturates the nation's air
And soils the peace of saintlike men.

Tarry and sooty, the slag seeps to the marrow

Shakes the heavy weight to righteous jowls
With tremorous caw to rouse the morning sky—
The day's bitter news, alley fodder for the rats.

FOR WOMEN WHO CRUISE THE NIGHT

—after Terry Wolverton

alone you speed where nothing exists
broken glass explodes into glitter
the asphalt is scarred with the spin of your wheels
escaping the wallpaper and bad plumbing
driving wide-laned empty boulevards
north to south, east to west
whispers of smoke climb the air from the bright ends
of your eyes—headlights or stars
maps dissolve at the mouth of nostalgia
your hair and arms wind-kissed, bared & daring
the years screech & scream as you leave them behind
destination known as you traverse those inky ribbons of love
wary & slit-eyed
the prey that stalks its beast

—after C.D. Wright

we scrounge around a molehole
stinking of decay
we sleep in the coldest
part of the heart
we fuck in darkness
we hate under our breath
there's no poetry here
all the crystal stemware shards
most nights we stay up late
kept awake by bad gas

fear locks us together
creaking meat

—after Charles Wright

The eldest-born to them
Grows weedlike and mean,
Breezy summery days
Inviting her out to play.
But she's devoted to

Their past, the tending &
The mending—keeping old
Glories intact, collecting
The stories and chasing
Off spells of yellow.

You know her type, how she
Smiles easily at nothing,
Cries easily at less than
Nothing, clings to the
Imaginary like a broom.

From one corner of one
Room, the life refused sits
Down to dinner, crosses
Hairy stingy legs—wineglass
Emptied, demanding refill.

241

HAVING LOST MY SON, I CONFRONT THE WRECKAGE

—after James Wright

During dark,
on the borderline between sea & soul
I walk yesterday's path, hunting everywhere,
seeking to explore every light
walking corridors that close around me
like the birth of a pearl.

Behind a star
its light on the chilled rubble
of my city-bred heart:
Frost, frost.

This is where he has gone
stillborn, under the eaves.

Bundled away under waves and smiling faces.

Beyond sick, I go on
clawing earth, making brick,
erecting monoliths. Here, on these altars
all the urns,
all the lost hopefuls.

This cold summer
Sun spills inhuman snow
the jewels
of his tears burn my palms.

Living. He's living still. I will
not let him die!
I will not let his light escape
this beauteous ruin.

—after Adam Zagajewski

my fingers blaze/comets strike earth, explode
    in my bowels.
my heart recoils, my stomach roils. books rumble
    from the shelves
above me. i brood on how often they've
    failed me.
there's a flash! the anthologies open and poets
    nakedly true
rage in their visions/a chorus of roars. history
    opens. the bards
strike like Allied bombs raining on Dresden, targets
    illuminated
despite the density of ignorance. the worthy
    scatter-gun the
silence. yet this greedy conflict consumes them.
    they vanish
in the zone like whispers from deathcamp bunkers.

i count each drop of inspiration, compose
    diatribes and
curses, each word a blast. thoughts like snipers fire
    ceaselessly as
my imagination smites enemies and fools alike,
    slogging the
swamp of the fallen, in sludge to my hips, a shadow
    battling shadows.
hoarse cries rise noisily. the pages fill/reveal

my faith and my abysmal lust

—after Louis Zukofsky

we spark lights
inside one another

living/have loved will love
no one knows the truth
about love.
not all love is good
(then that ain't it,
some say,

obsession greed indulgence lust

all better words)
perhaps
it is an unexpected stranger
washing away apprehension
with rapt tongue

startling beasts from slumber
who roar their hunger
to the tireless stars,
those tiny eyes gathering visions
like fishermen casting for fish seaside

whatever we've recorded
one of the other
wonder is
there's still so learnable much

wherever we put our words is our poem

VI

A KINGDOM OF CLOUDS

outside, the stingy scrub promises a cosmic green
that never quite arrives. lilting voices rise,
flicker and fall along the hallways
of a faded peach interior. behind walls one
can hear the shifting of seasons, the distant
warning barks of a disturbed dog, and the whimpers
of a nipple-starved infant. miles above the roof, a pink
peppermint cloud is anchored before the sun. the rain
is kept in the closet. the moon is kept in
the refrigerator. under the bed, where the dragons
are hidden, the mattress reeks of August and failed magic

this is a gone golly place

Hi, Georgiana.

When you see Pop, tell him I said hello.

Just a few days ago I was recalling
him in the light of my near death. We
were once again standing off in the dark
stall of hospital admissions. It was
October, 1957. His 43rd birthday was days
away, as was my eleventh. And I was sick
with delusions and fever (you know, as
said elsewhere, they've never quite left me).
I was wrapped in my favorite heavy
blue blanket, pulled straight off the bed in
Mama's panic. I was in those blue and white
print flannel pjs Mama sewed. I was so sick
I couldn't stay awake, kept going in and out
of consciousness. I listened that night as
Pop and Mama desperately argued with the
White admissions nurse and begged her
that I be allowed to see a doctor. They just
didn't let any Negro child into the hospitals
in those days, especially if the physician
didn't oversee the admission himself. I can't
drive this city without thinking of Pop.

Tell him I'm sorry I haven't been able to
keep up the gravesite. Tell him I'm sorry
that things haven't worked out as I'd hoped.
Tell him I'm sorry that rent, food and
transportation are still the big issues. Tell him
that I know it's late and that I'm way overdue.

Yours,

my feet bite my ankles
as i exit damnation's bus, neuron deep
    in nagging
uncertainties expressed in a glimpse
associated with sorrow-sated orbs
my limp calculated to relieve pressure
on newly formed callus, funkiness rolling
earthward from my lids, evoking frequent blinks
and infected lash follicles

(mouth bound in perfect tension
My Love zips past me in a yellow taxi,
eyes firmly fixed on the godtwat)

there is no one home
nevertheless i'm westbourne & bound
driven by the imagined spread of cool nylon
    under my blessed bum
by imagined rescue from sneaker rub
and the cold quench of sugarless iced tea
    to mute
    the pearl-toned essence of corporate jizz

    i'm eyeballing
    the sizzling cement
    for my perfect Houdini
    for the perfect escape hatch
    in the welcome ground
    to open and swallow me whole

May the sky widen between your eyes
and a storm twist across your thoughts.

May the false images you create devour all you
give birth to. May the false images you worship obscure love.

May you look in the mirror and see the malignancy.

May you writhe in dishonor. May you writhe hearing the
          voices
of those you have dishonored. May you writhe knowing the
whole of the pain you've caused others.

May the limitations you impose on those more gifted
than yourself steal the beats of your heart.

May you be kept out of the heaven
from which you have kept others.

May no one hear your last words.
May a small rodent eat your last words.

silence emerges as boundaries
and having
reached the beautifully wrapped bottom
is of no consolation as the floor gives way
to reveal yet another level to the plunge

(composed to Billy Idol singing
"White Wedding"... it's a niiiiice day to ...)

deep fall

to a truer South where the stomp of marching feet
is taken for the distant throb of conga drums

he kissed me but refused to hold my hand

depersonalized if preordained woo
non-hazardous biospatial corners sensate
with deceptive soothe & false croonings

thirty years of bleeding/the accidental history
of my memory in sanguine-stained vellum
all knocklubby & ooky as if stewed in butter

his name tattooed on my belly, lust striae
leaving me disfigured & pregnant with
strategies for impending wars

he kissed me but refused my hand

color is a language

otherwise, i could have been anyone i wanted

1. Rebirth

Baudelaire writes from his study.
In this incarnation he is twenty-two
and has only recently discovered his might.
He is intoxicated with the power
of poetry in the millennium of its
aesthetic decline. He is attending
graduate school in the U.K. and while
visiting Wales, pens desperate
letters to foreign poets he fancies—
to other visionaries in other lands.
This new world is a dreamer's
dessert, the possibilities for perversion
and privation and passion and purity
so much greater. The tragedies enormous on
such a global scale. He admires
Rimbaud (and himself, of course
since he is the greatest poet who
ever lived) and is planning soon to translate
himself anew. And perhaps explore the
voices of the Americas. Someday
soon, they will know him by this virgin
nom de plume. The songs of this time
to burn as brightly in his fire and all of
poetry's light the spill of his desire.

2. Discovery

Synthetic fabrics decay quickly,
a ruin agitated by her soft fleshy warmth.
She shuns daylight, not because
of preference for night, but because there

are fewer eyes to violate her darkness.
What shall she wear, other than the choicest
whispers/designs coutured by griefsmiths
fitting tightly at the throat and groin?
A yolk of lace or a noose of silk. Lately,
word has reached her of watchers hoping to
catch her nude and ravished and choking
on a spoon, graceless in her strangulation.
Unshockable, yet sad, she laughs them off.
Blends of fine cottons pulled, polished and
printed to a pearl-like sheen absorb the ink
of her imaginings and the stains of her
regurgitations. She visits the Pacific again,
to swim in her torment, this time driving a
new sedan, wearing the rags and weight
of a former marriage, the roar of rock 'n' roll
full volume, chain-smoking cigarettes, watching
the gulls, the thunderheads, the waves. This,
she decries, is the brink of communication.
    Below, the torrents.

3 . Artistic fusion

Certain symptoms become evident
with each intervening crisis.
The degree of responsiveness
on the part of the lover is questioned,
as is the beloved's ability to achieve the proper
tone elicited. In this test, the subject must
supply the appropriate touch to complete a feeling.
The mutual interdependence between the two
should result in a meaningful percept.

this terrible good between us

dizzy with kiss
sickened by roses

>   slowness is congenital
>   trash repudiates refinement
>   every sound a manifesto
>   danger creates movement

cut them just above the heart
with a fairly heavy but very sharp tool
let memory bleed

Easter Sunday. i tally hurts in a splash
of dreams, tremble with recriminations

these ravings of one wounded

i will mention names
rat out the rats
release the horror plague of details
bore them with the blood
of victims
each death toward the sum of the world

mother is why i do mother is what i do
i revise myself as i reveal myself

(image)

this expression of my reality as i feel it
a push against what contains me
i imagine the possibility of recognition

i imagine saving my own life

a cloud the size & density of a nation
obscures my beauty. in this scenario
i am the beast
throbbing in a den of bones

a petulant stubborn radiance spoils my darkness
light. everywhere.
i cannot bear his brightness. yet, without it
my once-savored cold becomes
a soul-rending ache

loving him leaves me cracked, swollen & akimbo

shortly before sunrise, i become the creature
i really am—a domesticated purr
no longer strutting & prowling for
the sake of thrillchasers—cozy, claws retracted,
in the confines of a quilted familiarity

a prison of diverse drives & revenge fantasies

pale golden sheets & pillows
turning over in them i inhale his scent
the ruined years, the bad behaviors
the threats the violences the couplings

the laws of sleep
govern this arousal
an uneasy somnambulance/a language
of snores & open-mouthed gaspings for wakefulness

i call your name. i call your name

---

the beast addresses her beauty

"i hate Sundays when you stand me
up. i am deliberately left out of everything.
i use my perfume to get rid of your stinkings.
my eyes are dull and bloodshot. i am sick
of mutants like you, silly to the last syllable,
bogus to the bootleather."

---

mirror. you again

---

the black sports car runs over a dog in the fog

it is silent on the rooftops of officeland
the slick weatherproofed windows of gross blue
design reflect nothing

my brother is burning prison cells and praying someone
will recognize his greatness

i cannot afford sleep. i've been priced out of my bed

the fog settles on the shoulders of my lover. his
face is a map of the city i drive

the sports car is spinning on its tires. the dog spasms
and cries

write to me, baby. send money & dreams

imagine the sheet is a canvas
you paint me. now, make the bed.
now turn back the quilt

i am on my back. you have put me here
we feel as if we are cheating on one another. we are
doing it every afternoon.

we are guilty teenagers after school
we will dance like this until the day we die

in the alley it is time to roll the dice
and quit jivin'. bad company with a short dog in his
black sports jacket. sterno on the brain

    (standing alone in the emptiness, the heat
      rises from between my corpulent thighs, eats the
      crotches out of all my slacks
      when i patch them it devours the patches)

i want to return to Sydney and drive Bondi Beach
i want to sample my home sounds Blarney-style
i want to see Paris while i still have eyes

he's inside my body. therefore, i cannot hide
the fact that my mind
is elsewhere. it is seated at the
dining table, addressing envelopes and licking stamps

a napkin full of lovejuices

a sweat-drenched sepia femininity trapped in his
amber & emerald seduction

hands like busy gophers burrow for moonstone

the night the fog the stink of an ashtray
cluttered with cigarette butts the blasting of
a soulful, "say you will, say you will ..."
the lonely black GM sports coupe hugging deserted corners

i am on my back. you put me here

i am stuck in the Hollywood of the seventies

---

it has been dictated that the passionate & amorous be killed

(meanwhile, in another part of the wound)

drowning. foam & flotsam. the last thing i see
is the hand of a friend.

why push me under?

what i see is the smile of a lover

what i see is my mother. see, i say, you've made
me wet my pants.

a colleague offers a lifeline then snatches it away
"but i am drowning" i cry

"drown then," they all say. "drown then fool. in that ocean/
all you believe."

---

there were millions waiting for genesis on earth
you tasted me and i tasted you

we promised we would meet even if that intertwining
took the culmination of a thousand dyings

but we did not know about forgetfulness, how it is fed
through an umbilicus

how the sky and clouds and stars are
made of it. how amnesia is a kingdom unto itself.

i did not remember that if i stood still long enough
in the swim and tide of discontent, time would bring you
crashing into my lap with the onrush of water

---

there is a special kind of forgetting
it makes the stars go away. the moist lips and

pleading eyes of other lovers pale to
invisibility, the sweat from their palms

dries into a salt against the skin
and is rinsed away in rivulets of wind

their seed becomes crows dancing on utility lines

it makes an oxymoron of wise experience. it
makes the lonely eye read joy into pained text

o bittersweet amnesia. as subtle as the tingle
that lingers during afterplay

> fingers kissing eyes/the black & white
> of it/a blood sonata/verse
> never-mailed letters to very important phonies

---

mirror. me again

---

stage of strange weather

apply for his social security benefits
no one returns your calls. mad fax till
they threaten your arrest for harassment

stage of grief

coax the medical facility into
complete examination even though you know
they don't want to treat your kind of people

stage of preparation

deal with his friends who didn't know
mama was so black nigger black
omit relatives of white lover who did

stage of grief

deal with everyone who blames you alone
deal with the rage of so-called friends
who abandoned you as the need awakened

stage of immense rain

give away his things for keepsakes
store his clothes nearby. integrate
his household items into yours

stage of grief

frame a photo. burn a candle on all holy days

stage of chaos

there is no one to do anything for you except you

>   forget how you mistook the tumors for monkey bites.
>   forget the wall of indifference
>   the wall of helplessness
>   forget the unvented rage. forget years
>   of unkept promises. forget every breath

remember him as he reappears in your dreams

---

we are lucky not to know. our hands must
relearn it from the start. as must our legs.
even our toes. our lips are lucky because they
are always hungry. just like our ever-reaching
and unfillable arms. we are lucky. to know each
other is to know constant rediscovery. i find you.
you find me. we are the lucky ones. we must relearn
all the things we once knew—kicking, screaming,
crying and, of course, the proper way to laugh

---

we kept inside the boundaries made of flesh
i did not know you then. i did not know

what it was like to walk the pier at sunset
and gaze at seabirds hovering overhead, snatching
bread from the fingers of tourists. i did not know

what it was like to hold a willing hand, one
that ached for my clasp. your hand. the salt of
you eating away my delicate darkness. i did not know

that lust, too, becomes finer and deeper as it ages

---

thoughts on water

i am my mother's rhythm

boiling. in the kitchen
i boil eggs. two minutes. firm whites
with just-set yellows. boiling inside

i am founding member of
the club for sensitive idiots.
i look perfectly normal
on the outside and wise. but

i have forgotten my own name. and where
my heart is hidden has become a mystery.

i used to like to walk down the middle of the street
braving traffic. i still do. like a daredevil
who fears nothing but erasure.

i scrawl everything down
am apt to forget the unwritten.

like the color of your thighs, the layers
of your smile. the tickle of your
mustache when you bury your head in my beard

---

walker at 3 a.m. in the morning. walker
think out frustrations. walker, invite
the unknown out of the shadows and into your soul

flaming with disappointment, at free burn

forget that reckless drive nowhere
burning rubber, burning tobacco,
burning all toll bridges to the past

those tracks laid out from feet to horizon
spread your legs across them, cup your breasts

straddle the impact

> *no native sky protected me*
> *no lover's love shielded my heart*
> *i fell slave to the common sorrow*

262

survivor of this century, this city

"they have not skill enough my worth to praise"

departed senses. brainfingers
worked to the heartbone. the rose of your sacrifice
soaked into the ground

no apologies forthcoming. strength
squandered in ceaseless efforts to prove
oneself worthy of a not-so-humble attention

(refusing to take the job that could fill
the pockets while the despoilers ransack the spirit)

beneath the nightshirt everything in ruins

---

mirror. is that you?

---

there are no recordings of my father's
voice. yet i hear him every day
he speaks to me
that's a good girl, he says.
don't worry needlessly.
stuff like that. his words are clear
despite the soft thickness
of his huge mahogany lips. the words
rumble. not so much like thunder
as like a train.
when he was happy, it took on a
sweetness. it went upregister when he
got angry and constricted to a silence
when he slapped or spanked us
determined to give us what was good for us so that we

would obey. like it said in the bible. as
per the commandments of that other
more merciless parent
there are no recordings of my father's
voice. yet i hear him every day

---

there are so many endless clamorings

there has been a drowning. multitudes
face-up, carried on the river

i seek one face. my likeness.

---

    the boy and the girl
my beloved children. sleep's moisture crusted
in the corners of their eyes and mouths.
my beloved children who inspire mama (alone, now) to
tolerate the derision and contempt of bosses,
the ugly silences of coworkers and the suspicions
of bureaucrats. my beloved children with frowns
on their faces wishing for waffles instead
of cold fruit and hard half-burned toast
(most of the burned part scraped off) still
in their pajamas, shivering in the morning's cold
because we must save the heat for a more terrible
cold. beloved children clutching their spoons, rubbing
their feet together, arms clamped to sides. my beloved
children lovely with faith that mama will succeed
    the boy and the girl

last night. reading them into a dream state

this is my sorrow song

---

stepping thru one mirror after another

---

my stories begin, reach climax yet go unfinished

there are no stars in my moonless sky

i know nothing of pine forests or
finely leaded translucence

a cold plunge into the cool flow of the river
is something i will never take

lovely cliffs & the dwellings of fishermen
escape my canvas

yet, i feel no longings for evocations of Harlem rebirths
or warm sorghum over hot-buttered biscuits

 the telltale red stains
 on the white enamel beneath my wrists
 are blobs of ketchup
 scraped from dinner plates

i am blowing my trumpet in a hurricane

this is what i do in my spare time

---

 she dreamed
spotted geckos lapping her toes
 she dreamed
lewd jokes & cold porridge
 she dreamed
small white nests filled with spiders
 she dreamed

guerillas liberating her from the tyranny of rust
    she dreamed
Christmas, Hollywood, 1976
    she dreamed
scales, chains and ruptured hopes
    she dreamed
fingers poking deep for malignancies
    she dreamed
glowing waters and sparkling boulders
    she dreamed
he pieced together the tatters of her mind
    she dreamed
they climbed down from the trees
    she dreamed
surrender to tender needy ghosts
    she dreamed
everything depended on her
    she dreamed
no world would allow her to land
    she dreamed
of eyes that were walls keeping her out
    she dreamed
the sky fell into her cup and sweetened her coffee
    she dreamed
she was the first of a new species
    she dreamed
of her son crying for her milk

---

the clouds hide nothing

her feet are bigger than his

there was no escape in today's mail

firm lips/a refusal to accept defeat

the cougar is silent in the soul

only the mud envies the stone

she passed thru heaven on her way

shepherdess or she-wolf?

there was a strange knock. the mountain appeared at the
        door

---

bad sugar/descendant of lightning bolts & lava flows

difficult days go by
i curse your name, grandfather
when clutching my chest
i feel you mother
        poverty
threatening to snatch back the cheapness
of your blessing

i have forgotten my name

heart. gone. mystery

1

smudged fingerprints

cheap water-based paint, lust ten layers deep
over and over the walls speak
voices clear and without accent tell me
what one so-called friend kept secret
a terrible penalty will be paid for trust
(o and to think i brought it into the
house)
who was the Hecuba who believed good potlikker
could rule out genetic predisposition
and nullify cradle-to-grave social abuse?
who was the Hecuba who could

2

midnights bring on poisoned sleep
spells for success fail
and a wedding day bodes an abiding and
relentless bleeding. downfall will
come with the muted cries of lock-key kids
his pleasure restricted to the pursuit of
his dope-fed illusions & her deluded belief
that not only can she overcome adversity,
but bad advice and the jealousy of knaves.
their journey is a shock-ridden careen
through a wasteland of slashed wrists,
amphetamines and unscratchable itches.
their deep-Hollywood story will
come to its predictable ending: the rape
of beauty, a secret bludgeoning, the
death of an angel

3

but when this grim heart
slips into its grimmer past
of terror shame rage
where broken dreamless nights
are interred, there is no relief
in pretense. fantasy is an affront.
ordinariness was wanted yet denied. what
was never learned in time proved the
undoing. mind be still. the crack-up
intensifies these recollections,
resurrects the flood of a bitter spring

4

you know it's your fault you
kept doing it when you should've
stopped. you squandered irretrievable
bliss. you. the reason of you the
mirror says you, the highball glass contains
you, your face floats up from the ash and
smoke at the end of this cigarette.
the clock spun backwards around you.
from behind the closed door out you stepped. you.
under the merciless light you were revealed
these are the dark currents in which
you do the butterfly stroke upstream. you. so
rude & tender & strong. you are a guardian,
no, a watcher, no, a warden. you are what was
so dearly paid for. you are the gas pedal
to the floor. your beauty is a maker of
myths. on your tongue piss turns to milk

you devastate me

269

do not remember. forget

a dream among objects

outside that closed door of
the rosewashed room, framed
against the doorway, a Queen Anne chair
the sitter waits in shadow

we did not meet. there was
no entanglement of tongues
i did not experience love
race did matter
and my hymen did not break
you were unconcerned about impressing
anyone, least of all my parents
our stars did not cross
there is nothing to the past

forget my name

Printed April 2001 in Santa Barbara &
Ann Arbor for the Black Sparrow Press by
Mackintosh Typography & Edwards Brothers Inc.
Text set in ITC New Baskerville by Words Worth.
Design by Barbara Martin.
This first edition is published in paper wrappers;
there are 300 hardcover trade copies;
125 hardcover copies have been numbered &
signed by the author; & 22 copies lettered A–V
with an original line drawing by Wanda Coleman
have been handbound in boards by Earle Gray
& are signed by the author.

Photograph: Heather Harris

WANDA COLEMAN was born in 1946 and raised in the Los Angeles community of Watts, famed for its August 1965 rebellion. Following this ethnic insurrection she joined a teenpost and a number of organizations set up to channel "the riotous" energies of young Black Americans into constructive modes. As a struggling young welfare mother, she was determined to become a writer. She has worked as a medical secretary, magazine editor, journalist and scriptwriter. She subsequently received literary fellowships from the National Endowment for the Arts and the Guggenheim Foundation for her poetry. Her honors in fiction include a fellowship from the California Arts Council and the 1990 Harriet Simpson Arnow Prize (from *The American Voice*). She received the 1999 Lenore Marshall Poetry Prize for *Bathwater Wine* (1998) from the Academy of American Poets, *The Nation* magazine and the New Hope Foundation. She is the author of *Imagoes* (1983), *Heavy Daughter Blues: Poems & Stories 1968-1986* (1987), *A War of Eyes & Other Stories* (1988), *African Sleeping Sickness* (1990), *Hand Dance* (1993), *Native in a Strange Land: Trials & Tremors* (1996), *Mambo Hips & Make Believe: A Novel* (1999) and *Mercurochrome* (2001), all published by Black Sparrow Press.